Praise for *Creative Disruption*

'Simon Waldman brings invaluable retrospective clarity to the turbulent effects of the internet so far. He doesn't claim to know where it's taking us next, but rightly warns of dramatic change ahead. Anyone who reads this book carefully will be far better equipped to take advantage of the unexpected and far less likely to make the same mistakes again.'

Sir Martin Sorrell, CEO WPP

'What should a business do when it finds itself shaken to the core by the internet? The answers to this question are too often simplistic, or laden with doom. Simon Waldman offers a different approach by offering sensible advice, grounded in business reality and fuelled by real insight into what the internet can and can't do.'

Luke Johnson, chairman of Risk Capital Partners and the RSA

'Simon Waldman really understands the internet. He shows a profound grasp of the options open to businesses that have been disrupted by the internet. He writes with clarity and impact, combining personal experience with highly relevant case studies. The end result is a book full of sound strategic and operational advice.'

Paul Myners, former chairman of Marks & Spencer

Creative disruption

FT Prentice Hall
FINANCIAL TIMES

In an increasingly competitive world, we believe it's quality of thinking that gives you the edge – an idea that opens new doors, a technique that solves a problem, or an insight that simply makes sense of it all. The more you know, the smarter and faster you can go.

That's why we work with the best minds in business and finance to bring cutting-edge thinking and best learning practice to a global market.

Under a range of leading imprints, including *Financial Times Prentice Hall*, we create world-class print publications and electronic products bringing our readers knowledge, skills and understanding which can be applied whether studying or at work.

To find out more about Pearson Education publications, or tell us about the books you'd like to find, you can visit us at **www.pearsoned.co.uk**

Creative disruption

What you need to do to shake up your business
in a digital world

Simon Waldman

Financial Times
Prentice Hall
is an imprint of

Harlow, England • London • New York • Boston • San Francisco • Toronto
Sydney • Tokyo • Singapore • Hong Kong • Seoul • Taipei • New Delhi
Cape Town • Madrid • Mexico City • Amsterdam • Munich • Paris • Milan

PEARSON EDUCATION LIMITED

Edinburgh Gate
Harlow CM20 2JE
Tel: +44 (0)1279 623623
Fax: +44 (0)1279 431059
Website: www.pearsoned.co.uk

First published in Great Britain in 2010

© Pearson Education 2010

The right of Simon Waldman to be identified as author of this work has been
asserted by him in accordance with the Copyright, Designs and Patents Act 1988.

Pearson Education is not responsible for the content of third party internet sites.

ISBN: 978-0-273-72573-2

British Library Cataloguing-in-Publication Data
A catalogue record for this book is available from the British Library

Library of Congress Cataloging-in-Publication Data
Waldman, Simon.
  Creative disruption : what you need to do to shake up your business in a digital
world / Simon Waldman.
    p. cm.
  Includes index.
  ISBN 978-0-273-72573-2 (pbk.)
  1. Creative ability in business. 2. Electronic commerce. 3. Success in business.
  I. Title.
  HD53.W354 2010
  658.4'063--dc22

                                   2010029932

10 9 8 7 6 5 4 3 2 1
14 13 12 11 10

Typeset in 10pt Plantin by 3
Printed by Ashford Colour Press Ltd, Gosport

For Gay Waldman

1945–2009

Contents

About the author

Simon Waldman started his career as a journalist specialising in retail, media and technology. In 1993, he took his first steps online, and has been obsessed with the internet and its impact on business and society ever since. He spent 14 years at Guardian Media Group, first as editor of their websites, and ultimately as director of digital strategy and development and during this time became acknowledged as one of the world's leading thinkers on the evolution of the media industry.

He is a former chair of the UK's Association of Online Publishers, and a non-executive director of the Nordic's leading directory business, Eniro. His current day job is group product director at one of Europe's leading subscription entertainment businesses, LOVEFiLM. His blog to accompany this book can be found at www.creativedisruption.net. When time permits, he tweets as @waldo.

Acknowledgements

This book simply could not have been written without the support and encouragement of my former boss, Carolyn McCall. In so many ways, I couldn't have done it without her.

Similarly, I have to thank the *Guardian*'s editor-in-chief, Alan Rusbridger for his tireless championing of the digital cause, and creating an environment where online creativity and innovation could flourish.

There isn't space to thank individually all the colleagues within Guardian Media Group who have helped me learn the lessons that were the spark for this book. But Steve Folwell, Sybil Carolan, Chris J Wade, and Sarah Pobereskin who sat near me throughout this book's development, deserve a special mention, for having to listen to each anecdote as I discovered it, and providing vital feedback on the early drafts. Also, I could not have juggled the process of research and writing with my day job without the tireless support of Lisa Rout, Helen Dagley and Hayley Kimpton.

Many people gave their time to help me shape my vague ideas into something approaching a coherent argument. Some are quoted on these pages, others provided vital feedback, background and insight but have not been mentioned. To this end, I would particularly like to thank Saul Klein, Brent Hoberman, Judy Gibbons, Stefan Glaenzer, Paul Zwillenberg, Julian Birkinshaw, Jeremy Silver, Peter Read, Christian Sandstrom, Alice Enders and Doug McCabe of Enders Analysis, and Ollie Purnell of Q5 for their help.

For challenging my preconceptions about the publishing industry, I am hugely grateful to Genevieve Shore of Pearson, Sara Lloyd at Pan Macmillan and Simon Juden of The Publishers Association.

I have to thank Mark Read of WPP for organising the fantastic Stream un-conference that provided huge inspiration and a first oppor-tunity to air some of the ideas that ended up on these pages. Similarly I owe much to all the team at Burda whose DLD events provided a feast of food for thought.

I will not pretend to have seen further than others that have gone before me, but for many of the ideas in this book I am certainly standing on the shoulders of giants. Clayton Christensen's work on 'disruptive technology' gave me the framework to see that what was happening in the newspaper industry was not an isolated case. The title is a reworking of Joseph Schumpeter's 'creative destruction' and although I read plenty of his work, it was only after reading Thomas McCraw's excellent biography, *Prophet of Innovation*, that I began to understand its relevance.

I also have to thank my spectacularly patient editor, Christopher Cudmore, who put up with my countless missed deadlines and gently nudged my rambling prose into something that I hope you find worth reading.

Last and definitely not least, I have to thank my wife, Suzanne, for putting up with the weekends and evenings I was locked away writing, and the spectacular grumpiness that can hit a first-time author with half a book left to write. Don't worry, there won't be a sequel …

Publisher's acknowledgements

We are grateful to the following for permission to reproduce copyright material:

Figures
Figure 6.1 from United Business Media, http://www.ubm.com/ubm/ir/presentations/2010/2010-03-05a/2010-03-05a.pdf, page 3; Figure 6.2 from Google Finance.

Text

Newspaper headline on page 81 from 'HMV and a wily Fox have defied the pundits', *The Times*, 02/07/2009 (Dunne, H.), © *The Times* and 02.07.2009/ nisyndication.com

In some instances we have been unable to trace the owners of copyright material, and we would appreciate any information that would enable us to do so.

Introduction: OMG! The internet ate my business

n February 1996, I walked into the *Guardian*'s offices to do my first day's work on some of the company's first websites. I was 30 years old, a half-decent journalist and utterly obsessed with the internet.

The *Guardian* had always been *the* newspaper for me. It was left-leaning. It had the best writers, brilliant arts coverage and a reputation for creativity and innovation. I had read it since I'd been a student; and, for a journalist like myself, who had started on the trade press (*Shoe and Leather News* was my beginning), getting a job there was all I could have dreamed of.

Were it not for my internet obsession, however, I would never have stood a chance. Competition was fierce, and I was neither talented nor pushy enough to get anywhere near the front of the queue. But in those early days of the internet, knowledge of the online world was thin on the ground, and I had just about enough to be of use to them. So, here I was heading up to the fourth floor of a disused warehouse that was home to the *Guardian*'s New Media Lab.

This was a *cool* office. As was the fashion at the time, everyone wore combat trousers and trainers. Drum-and-bass played non-stop over the stereo. People smoked at their desks. Everyone was young. It was half workplace; half nightclub. Incredibly, they were paying me to be here.

That day was the start of 14 phenomenal years at the crucible of internet-driven change in the newspaper industry. As my career progressed – moving from journalism to management; from management to the board; and on to a strategy role in our group HQ – so did the internet's impact on our business: both for better and worse.

Everywhere we looked online there were opportunities: we could respond to the news immediately; use audio and video; and engage with users from around the world. The number of people visiting our site went from hundreds of thousands, to millions, and to tens of millions. And so, eventually, did our online revenues. We had greater online reach than newspapers with ten times our daily readership in print. We picked up awards by the truckload, and an international reputation as a newspaper that had got the internet right.

Over time, the organisation changed. The internet moved from being something that happened in a warehouse across the road to being an integral part of all the different bits of our business: from how we sold advertising, to how we decided about which story to publish and when. In 2005, it became policy to put the next day's stories onto the website before they appeared in print. And when we moved into new offices at the end of 2008, print and online journalists sat together around an integrated news desk nicknamed 'the knuckleduster'.

But if the internet gave with one hand, it took away with the other. Initially, we saw money flooding into our newspapers as one venture-capital backed start-up after another used our pages to attract customers, and recruit staff. But over time, that money started to shift online – to Google and to online job boards – and so ultimately did many of our print readers and advertisers.

In line with the rest of the industry, circulation gradually slipped away. In February 1996 it hovered at around 400,000, by February 2010 it had dipped below 300,000 (although during that time the cover price had increased from 40p to £1). But the real financial wound came from the decline of classified advertising in print – in our case, for job advertising.

Over the years, tens of millions came off the top line of the business, first as companies started to shift money online and then as they slowed down their hiring efforts altogether because of the recession. Growth in online revenues was good – but not good enough to compensate for this – and our cost base now had to carry a fully fledged digital operation as well as the traditional infrastructure required to get a national newspaper out seven days a week, 52 weeks a year.

In 2009, we announced significant losses; and an equally significant wave of restructuring and redundancies as a result. The *Guardian*, as I'll discuss later, is ultimately owned by a trust – and therefore immune from short-term shareholder pressures. However, it can only sustain a certain loss for a certain amount of time,[1] and thanks to the combination of the internet and the fiercest recession in living memory, it had crossed the line.

As I left the business in 2010, the same fundamental challenges remained: the need to build the digital business and sustain the print business for as long as possible; to continue to invest in quality journalism when we will face real challenges on the business's top line for years to come, and the need to compete effectively in the world of online advertising dominated by Google, Microsoft, Yahoo! and a host of big, global networks.

There is no simple solution. The *Guardian* had done a much better job than many others – but the hard maths of the situation remained challenging and will, I suspect, remain so for many years to come.

---

1 The quality end of the UK's national newspaper market consists primarily of loss-making titles supported by protective owners: *The Times* has lost money for decades and is kept afloat by Rupert Murdoch; the *Independent* has never made a profit since its launch and in 2010 became the second loss-making UK paper in the Russian oligarch Alexander Lebedev's stable; and the *Guardian* having been profitable at the end of the 20th century has made a loss since 2001/02.

From living it, to writing about it

This book is not the story of my time at the *Guardian*, but it has been fundamentally shaped by it. It comes from a combination of a fascination with the new, and the coal-face experience of trying to reinvent and transform the old. Above all, it comes from realising that the challenges and opportunities we faced at the *Guardian* were not unique. And it wasn't just other newspapers that were going through the same things, but a host of different businesses in different sectors around the globe.

Three businesses first caught my eye. The most obvious was Encyclopaedia Britannica, which had been initially ravaged by Encarta and then by Wikipedia. Then came Kodak, which had seen its film business collapse at the start of the 21st century as a result of the arrival of the digital camera – even though Kodak itself invented the world's first digital cameras in its labs. Then came HMV, the entertainment retailer that most of the UK's adult population grew up buying vinyl, CDs, videos, DVDs and computer games from, and which had been hammered first by the arrival of Amazon, and then by both legal and illegal music downloading.

❝ no-one really seemed to offer any solutions ❞ In each case there was plenty written about where the old management had gone wrong, and much about what they should have done a decade or more ago – much of which was way, way too simplistic. For all the punditry, no-one really seemed to offer any practical solutions to a set of hellishly difficult predicaments. I wanted to take a look at these businesses in more detail. If after everything they had been through, and with the odds so firmly stacked against them, they had managed to get something right, then there had to be lessons we could learn.

In all three cases there were successes that could be emulated. Britannica, while a much smaller business than it had been, was now profitable and growing. At HMV, a new chief executive, Simon

Fox, was delivering sales growth for the first time in years. And while Kodak remains one of the most challenged businesses in town, it has made massive strides in moving away from its consumer film business (with sales of $10bn in 1993 and $500m in 2009) and was gradually reinventing itself as a predominately digital imaging business.

My investigation went further. I took a place on the board of Eniro, the leading directories business in the Nordic countries and saw many of the same challenges of transformation there. I started to investigate postal services, record labels, travel agents and even the porn industry – and again, similar themes began to emerge.

All these companies were dealing with the fact that the business models and ways of working that brought success for much of the 20th century were not capable of carrying them forward into the 21st century. Yes, there is an exciting digital world out there, but it brings with it new challenges, new competition, and none of the certainties that their traditional business has been built on.

A name for 'it': creative disruption

I needed something that summed up this phenomenon that was now starting to obsess me. The first word that kept coming into my head to describe this was 'disruption', as defined by the Harvard Professor, Clayton Christensen, in his excellent books *The Innovator's Dilemma* and *The Innovator's Solution*. I had read these books years earlier and found their description unbelievably relevant to what was happening to newspapers. According to Christensen, great companies often fail when confronted with 'disruptive innovations' that change the rules of competition in their markets. Often this is done by introducing products which incumbents think are sub-standard, but which in fact open up a whole new market.

Think how mainframe computers were toppled by the PC: many mainframe manufacturers just viewed PCs as toys for hobbyists. Likewise Nintendo's Wii disrupted the computer games market taking

50% market share by making games that were simple and fun for the whole family, while the Xbox and PlayStation focused on games that were ever more realistic, cost ever more to make and demanded greater and greater processing power.

The internet was sparking off disruptions all over the place: eBay was disrupting traditional retailing; MP3s were disrupting the music market; digital photography was disrupting film; blogs were disrupting journalism; and Google's text ads were disrupting the advertising world. Christensen's books weren't written about the internet, but they seemed to have been brought to life by it.

But disruption is not an automatic process, it has to start somewhere, or rather, be started by someone. The parallel trend was that some phenomenal businesses were being created. Google, Amazon, eBay, Skype, Netflix, Salesforce.com, Expedia, Net-a-Porter, Betfair and more recently Facebook and Twitter. They were either, like Amazon, taking a traditional business and completely reinventing it, or like Google, creating something that would previously have defied description.

❝ behind the success is a remarkable tale of entrepreneurship ❞

To see these businesses as simply 'disruptive' is far too blinkered: behind the success of each of them is a remarkable tale of entrepreneurship, often the result of one or two individuals who succeeded where thousands of others tried and failed. Not only that, but the collective experience of so many businesses going through so much change at the same time created a phenomenon of its own. It felt to me that there was something much bigger going on than the experience of any one business or industry. This wasn't just 'disruption' but a particular type of disruption happening at a particular time. What's more, as the mobile internet started to take off – and the generation that had grown up entirely online was starting to take its place in the workforce – it became all too clear that there was still plenty of change to come. So, Christensen was a good start, but I needed a little more to really sum up the enormity of what I believed was happening around me.

As I was searching for quotes about how the internet had changed the world of business the phrase that felt most right to me was 'a new physics of business', meaning a change in the rules of who can compete with whom, where and how. But I was hoping to find a quote that was slightly more apt. Eventually, I found the most perfect description. The internet, it said:

upsets all conditions of location, all cost calculations, all production functions within its radius of influence; and hardly any 'ways of doing things' which have been optimal before remain so afterward.

I loved the description of 'hardly any ways of doing things which have been optimal before remain so afterward' – it summed up perfectly the experience of all of the challenged businesses I was looking at with a conciseness and sense of understatement that is rarely found in commentators of the internet. Hardly surprising, as it happened: it turned out that this description wasn't written about the internet at all, it was written about the arrival of the railways in 1936 by the Austrian born economist Joseph Schumpeter, in his classic work *Business Cycles*.

Schumpeter is best known for his theory of creative destruction, which he believed was an inevitable part of capitalism. Progress for him came about as a result of 'new men' and 'new businesses' seizing upon advances in technology in order to create powerful new entities and new 'ways of doing things', which often result in the downfall or destruction of incumbents.

Schumpeter looked at massive waves of change, such as the impact the industrial revolution had on the textile industry or the impact of the arrival of the railways. As I read more and more of his work, it became clear that the internet was delivering a wave of change at least on a par with these earlier revolutions.

Schumpeter supplied the two pieces of definition that I felt Christensen was missing. First the idea that what we are living through is an era of change sparked by a technological leap – in our case the arrival of the internet and the digital world. Second he celebrated entrepreneurs and entrepreneurship. In fact he deliberately separated the technological innovation, and inventors, from the entrepreneurs who brought about the wave of massive change, and the end of many old ways of doing things.

This chimed with everything I had seen happen on the internet. As we see in Chapter 2, the story of the internet's impact on business is really the story of a relatively small number of entrepreneurs who have shaken up whatever industry they have touched, and created spectacular value as a result.

Schumpeter also captured the fury that overwhelmed tradesmen as they found themselves swept aside by these new men and their technologies; and the violence and legal wrangling that ensued. In the 16th and 17th centuries, craft guilds had new laws introduced and medieval regulations resuscitated in order to block innovation in the textile industry. In the 21st century, newspaper men have similarly hurled insults and sought legislative measures against Google, with even less success so far.

And so, with a nod to both Christensen and Schumpeter, I started to think of this as a period of several decades of new businesses emerging and traditional ones finding themselves profoundly challenged, or to put it more succinctly, an *era of creative disruption.*

What should we do about it?

Defining the problem is always helpful – but it is solving it that counts.

One's first reaction is to emulate the spectacularly successful businesses born out of the internet. There have been plenty of books written about the success of Google, Amazon, eBay, Facebook and Wikipedia, and deservedly so. These are some of the defining organisations of our era; they have created a new context that we all have to operate in. But if you are in a century-old business that is facing profound structural change, you have almost no corporate DNA in common with them and its ilk.

Those with a legacy business to manage – more specifically legacy businesses that are showing signs of internet-induced decline – face a particular set of challenges and need a particular set of solutions.

Stripped of the growth and strength they once knew, they have to reinvent themselves, often against a background of decline. The strategic, financial and human challenges are a million miles removed from Google wondering where its next billion dollar business will come from.

As well as looking at businesses facing such challenges here and now, I found a useful comparison by looking at two major turnarounds in the technology business. First of all, IBM's rebound from the biggest loss in corporate history in 1992, and the death of its core product, the mainframe, into the services and software giant that it has now become. There were lessons too from Apple – in particular the period that went from Gil Amelio becoming CEO in 1996 to Steve Jobs' delivering the ground-breaking iMac in 1998.

> there were lessons too from Apple

The one thing I didn't find was simple answers. If you are looking for silver bullet solutions, I'm afraid you will be disappointed. In fact, pretending that there are simple or painless solutions for businesses dealing with this kind of challenge is little short of neglect. My conclusion is that the only hope is a sustained process of reinvention that involves three parallel streams of activity.

- **Transform your core business:** stick to what you do, but reinvent how you do it – ruthlessly seek efficiencies, and create or bolt on innovating products, processes and services to ensure you can generate as much cash for as long as possible by doing what you know how to do best.

- **Find big adjacencies:** use your capabilities and assets to move into growth areas – without getting sucked into massive value-destructive mergers and acquisitions.
- **Innovate at the edges:** develop a tightly managed programme of relatively modest projects, investments or acquisitions, focused entirely on either developing products, services and processes that will feed back into your core business, or act as first tentative steps into what you hope will be major adjacencies.

The second half of this book looks at each of these three streams in turn, providing examples of what has worked and what hasn't, and what we can learn from them.

I don't pretend that I'm offering some sort of panacea here. As we will see, success for some businesses will still mean they end up smaller than they were a decade ago; and some will disappear altogether. A few will grow throughout the process but will experience tumultuous change along the way. It isn't quick. It isn't easy. And it isn't without pain. But, there is no alternative.

This book in bullet points

This book falls roughly into two parts. The first defines creative disruption, its causes and impacts; the second looks at what incumbent businesses have to do as a result. I finish with a look at what has happened to Kodak in the 15 years since it started taking digital imaging seriously; how creative disruption is about to hit the world of book publishing; and then take a brief look at the future.

It is a terrible thing to admit, but I can't remember the last time I read a business book cover to cover, so it's a bit rich to expect anyone who is reading this one to do exactly that. So before I start into the main chapters, here is a summary of the main arguments with references to the chapters that you can dip into if you want to know more.

◾ We are in the middle of an era of 'creative disruption'. This started with the launch of Mosaic, the first web browser in 1993, and is going to continue for at least another decade. See Chapter 2.

◾ The defining characteristic of creative disruption is the emergence of new businesses either providing something completely new for consumers (e.g. Google), or something traditional but in a radically improved or more efficient way (e.g. Amazon or Skype). The consequence for incumbent businesses is that they are faced with a stark choice of reinvention or oblivion.

◾ The term 'creative disruption' is a hybrid of Joseph Schumpeter's notion of 'creative destruction' and Clayton Christensen's work on 'disruptive innovation'.

◾ This change is happening in a host of different sectors at the same time, because the internet has created a new 'physics of business' – and with this the rules about who can compete in which market, and the rules of how they compete have been completely rewritten. See Chapter 2.

◾ For traditional businesses, the degree that this new physics affects you depends on whether your product has gone digital or whether it is just being purchased online. As newspapers, directories and the music industry have discovered, once your product goes digital your world is turned upside down. As the travel industry knows, if your product remains physical, intermediaries have to change how they operate or become irrelevant.

◾ The internet, however, doesn't drive change on its own – there are four forces that build on it to cause creative disruption (see Chapter 2):

  ◾ entrepreneurs and new entrants

  ◾ consumers' needs and desires

  ◾ the proliferation of connected devices

  ◾ economic volatility.

◾ There have been two phases of creative disruption; the third will start when the global economy returns to health, probably in 2012. It will involve the internet becoming increasingly mobile; televisions getting connected to the internet; an ever greater proportion of the world's population getting online; and a generation that has only known the internet starting to reach professional and economic maturity.

■ There are a number of things that any business faced with creative disruption needs to have in place right from the outset if their reinvention is to be a success. These include supportive owners, a healthy balance sheet, committed leaders, the right people in the business to drive a transformation, and a smart approach to cannibalisation. Without them, the challenge becomes increasingly difficult, if not insurmountable. See Chapter 4.

■ From looking at examples such as IBM, and Britannica and Apple (see Chapter 3), a disrupted business has to do three things if it is to successfully reinvent itself.

■ **Transform the core business (see Chapter 5):** the challenge here is to stick to what you do, but reinvent how you do it for the online age. This means continuous innovation and efficiency seeking. For HMV, it meant sorting out its physical stores to make the product mix more appealing. For IBM it meant reinventing the mainframe in order to sell at a much lower price while keeping up gross margins, and so providing the cashflow to build the software and services business that eventually saved the company. For newspapers, this means becoming much leaner organisations and a continuous rethinking of what content gets created, when and how.

■ **Find big adjacencies (see Chapter 6):** for some businesses, the process of core transformation might deliver long-term growth but very often it will result in swapping a high-margin business with strong barriers to entry for a low-margin business with weak barriers to entry. Real resilience, then, comes from using your capabilities to find new business areas that can offer secure growth.

This is how successful technology companies such as Cisco continuously evolve – aware that over time any technology will tend to become increasingly commoditised. It is also why the likes of Deutsche Post and TNT – national postal services – have moved into freight and logistics rather than pin all their hopes on cost cutting and the growth of e-commerce parcels to compensate for the decline in the number of letters being sent every year. It is also how Naspers, a South African newspaper business, has ended up being the largest shareholder in Tencent, China's leading social network, a stake they bought for $30m, but which by 2010 was worth more than $10bn.

■ **Innovate at the edges (see Chapter 7):** everyone loves to innovate, but in the context of a disrupted business, innovation – whether it is organic or through corporate venturing and taking small stakes in innovative start-ups – needs a clear focus. Its aim is pure and simple: either it is a way of creating the products, services and processes that will allow you to transform your core business, or it is a way of finding your footing as you search for a big adjacency. If it doesn't fit either of those criteria, you shouldn't be doing it. The biggest flaw a company can make is thinking that edge innovations alone will be enough. Big problems need big solutions – not an endless myriad of smart little initiatives.

■ Book publishers have the delights of two waves of reinvention: first as physical books started to be sold online and now with the rise of the Kindle, the iPad and a host of other readers, they are starting to see their product go digital. As we discuss in Chapter 9, they will see a wave of radical disruption as a result.

■ The future is going to be much closer to the chaotic dystopia of *Blade Runner* than the cartoon utopia of *The Jetsons*. As the economy recovers, the number of connected devices proliferate, and as we continue to spend more time and money online, the pace of creative disruption is only going to accelerate. Prolonged and painful transformations, such as that experienced by Kodak will become increasingly common. (See the Epilogue.)

2

The era of creative disruption

C reative disruption started in 1993, when Marc Andreessen, a 22-year-old student at the University of Illinois' National Centre for Super Computer Applications, created Mosaic – the first graphical web browser – and, in doing so, opened up the internet to the world.

The internet had already been around for 25 years, but was still predominately for academics and computer enthusiasts. The world wide web had been conceived by Tim Berners Lee two years earlier, but the first browsers were text based – designed primarily to let academics share information.

But with Mosaic, the web came to life – taking a first step towards the internet that people around the world experience today. The functionality was primitive compared to what we're used to today, but at the time it was a revelation. This is how *Wired* magazine described it:

Mosaic is the celebrated graphical 'browser' that allows users to travel through the world of electronic information using a point-and-click interface. Mosaic's charming appearance encourages users to load their own documents onto the Net, including colour photos, sound bites, video clips and hypertext 'links' to other documents. By following the links – click, and the linked document appears – you can travel through the online world along paths of whim and intuition.[1]

---

1 'The (Second Phase of the) Revolution Has Begun', *Wired*, October 1994.

Mosaic brought the web to the world, and the world to the web. It kick-started a radical transformation in how we communicate, how we gather information, and how we spend our time and our money. Before the launch of Mosaic, information technology had predominately allowed big businesses to get bigger. Through the 1970s and 1980s, airlines, publishers, retailers, broadcasters and banks all spent millions on big mainframe systems and data centres that helped them to become more efficient and expand across the globe.

As consumers, we felt some of the benefits of this technology indirectly, especially when it resulted in better products and lower prices – but this was *their* technology, not *ours*. Nowhere was this more visible than in the world of travel. The airlines developed online booking systems such as Sabre and Apollo which made the process of agents booking flights infinitely simpler. But as consumers we were cut off from it. When we went to a travel agent, it was *them* who went on the computer, we could only sit and watch.

Technological innovation in this period was good for business. It created barriers to entry, it drove out efficiencies, and it helped businesses that had been around for decades to experience dramatic surges in growth. Nowhere was this more true than the music industry, which gave us the CD in 1982 and which for nearly two decades experienced growth thanks to an increase in the price of new releases and a rejuvenation in back catalogue sales.

ff the web broke down barriers to entry 55

But as the web made its way into the world's homes and offices something started to change. Here was a technology that challenged big businesses rather than protected them. The web broke down barriers to entry rather than reinforced them. And it gave unprecedented technological power right into the hands of consumers.

Mosaic allowed the development of Travelocity, which meant that consumers could access travel booking information directly from their home. And after the music industry gave us the CD, we gave it the

MP3. Suddenly there were radical new ways of doing things in even the oldest of industries, and businesses emerged that simply couldn't have existed before. As Joseph Schumpeter said about the arrival of the railways: 'hardly any of the ways of doing things that had been optimal before remained so afterwards'.

The era of creative disruption had begun.

A new physics of business

The internet created a new physics of business: a fundamental change in the rules of who can compete with whom, and how and where they can compete. It allowed entrepreneurs to apply radical operating models to traditional businesses and to create businesses that simply couldn't have been conceived before. Consider these five examples:

▦ Craig Newmark can run Craigslist, which has classified sites in some 200 cities spread across six continents, with a few dozen staff in a suburb of San Francisco. His revenues – rumoured to be in the region of $100m – are staggering for a business that size, but are dwarfed by the $14bn dollars that have gone from US newspaper classified advertising partly as a result of Newmark and others like him.

▦ Salesforce.com has become a $1bn business offering customer relationship management (CRM) solutions to businesses that can be accessed by their employees wherever they are in the world, without them having to install any software on their PCs.

▦ Betfair has been able to create a completely new type of gambling company – an exchange that allows people around the world to bet against each other, rather than against it, and so dramatically reducing Betfair's risk. From their base in London, they have served more than 2 million customers around the world and in 2009 declared revenues of £303m and £38m in profits.

▦ In 2008, Tencent, the Chinese social networking site was able to generate $454m profit from $1bn revenues – a margin of 40% –

by selling virtual goods such as ringtones, and virtual bouquets of flowers or weapons for multiplayer games. At the time of writing, the business was growing at around 30% a year.

- Skype can operate as a global telecoms company, with paying customers around the world, serviced by only 320 staff. Its revenues – at around $500m in 2009 – are minute compared to any major telco, but its revenue per employee is approximately $1.7m. British Telecom's equivalent figure is around $300,000.

None of these businesses could have existed without the internet. They are all operating in ways that were simply impossible beforehand. Skype, Craigslist and Betfair have all redefined their sectors with radical operating models. Tencent meanwhile has created a business, quite literally, from thin air. But for many of those whose businesses started out in a pre-internet world, and who had reaped the benefits of an earlier wave of advances in IT, the consequences were often little short of traumatic.

Warren Buffet coined the term *economic moat* to describe the ability a company has to maintain competitive advantage over its rivals. The arrival of the internet saw a lot of economic moats being filled in.

- Those who were protected by geography – such as retailers or local media owners with a physical presence in a specific location – found themselves having to compete with businesses that could be based anywhere in the world.
- Those who create value through economic bundles, such as newspapers, CDs or TV channels, were challenged by disaggregation. Consumers could buy just the tracks they wanted from a CD rather than having to buy the whole album. Classified advertising services could exist on their own rather than depending on editorial to reach an audience.
- Those who acted as intermediaries found themselves potentially disintermediated as the internet enabled direct connections between proprietors and consumers. Even those who weren't disintermediated still had to compete with businesses born in

the digital age, operating with a fraction of the fixed costs, and therefore able to offer better prices to consumers and/or terms to their suppliers.

■ Those who were once protected by scarcity – particularly those who were once the creators of a product that had now been digitised – text, pictures, music, movies or directory listings – found themselves having to survive in a world where anyone can now create something similar and distribute it for themselves at minimal marginal cost.

The newspaper industry, where I worked from 1996, sat right in the middle of all of this. The likes of Monster, Auto Trader, Craigslist and eBay disaggregated our lucrative classified businesses from the editorial businesses they had supported. Having once been gatekeepers of news we found ourselves disin-termediated as Reuters and the Associated Press put their feeds on Yahoo! and MSN. Having once enjoyed scarcity – as one of a limited number of organisations that could create and distribute news

❝ we found ourselves operating in a world of bloggers ❞

– we found ourselves operating in a world of bloggers and passionate, well-informed amateurs. Those who once held strong regional and local franchises found themselves having to compete for readers and advertisers with the national and global brands mentioned above, not to mention a rather smart technology business called Google.

True, there have been creative opportunities aplenty, but our economic moats were systematically filled in. Little wonder the decade, compounded by a savage recession (a critical factor as we shall discuss later), has proved to be the most financially challenging in the industry's history. Structurally, the odds have shifted against us. In the US, newspaper advertising revenues dropped from $48bn to $37bn (a 25% decrease) between 2000 and 2008.[2] As a comparison, between 2001 and 2008 Google's revenues rose from $86m to $21.7bn (a massive 25,200% increase).

---

2 Newspaper Association of America advertising data.

And so we have the point and counterpoint of creative disruption: new businesses are appearing at a rapid rate of knots while traditional businesses find themselves facing profound structural challenges. Right across the economic spectrum, businesses of different sizes, shapes and in different sectors have been affected. With the advantage of hindsight, the trends seem clear – but as with any skirmish, when you're in the middle of it you can never quite see who is winning. Creative disruption arrived in 1993, but its impact was often anything but obvious, and certainly not evenly distributed.

In the early days of the internet – and the dotcom boom – the internet spawned a wave of businesses that promised to change the world, but delivered very little in profit as a result. Not only that but many of the businesses that were meant to be most challenged by the internet actually had a pretty good time during 2000. Traditional media was meant to be doomed, and so was traditional advertising, but there was a boom in both as venture capital backed businesses spent millions in print and TV trying to attract customers. Newspapers' classified advertising pages actually got thicker as the same start-ups tried to hire staff and an economic boom meant that property prices went through the roof. 2000 was a record year for US newspapers, a record year for CD sales, and a great year for high street retailers.

When the dotcom boom came to crashing halt, and one high profile start-up after another went to the wall, many traditional businesses felt they had seen off the internet; they and their investors believed business could continue as usual.

The *Guardian*'s economic editor, Larry Elliot, tells me there was a similar phenomenon at the arrival of the railways in the UK. It was meant to bring an end to the use of horses, but initially it resulted in dramatic growth in horse sales, as more people needed

" as the economy dipped people went online to find bargains "

transport to get to the railway stations. A short-term boom, however, masked a profound long-term shift. And so it was in our more recent scenario. Despite the boom up to 2000, as broadband penetration spread so did the amount of time and money that people spent online. As the economy dipped in 2001, people went online to find bargains. In 2002, Amazon declared its first profit and Google also started to become maddeningly profitable. The likes of Betfair, Saleforce, Craigslist and dozens of others all became real businesses, not just cash-burning proofs of concept. And so the maths of disruption that we saw above started to take place.

But exactly where creative disruption happens, and how severely it happens, is down to a number of factors: some relate to the intrinsic nature of individual businesses and industries; others are external factors. It is vital to understand these as we start to plot our paths for the future, and so this is where we turn our attention to next.

Three degrees of creative disruption

Different industries face three different degrees of disruption based on their inherent characteristics and how they are changed by this new physics of business.

1   Atoms to bytes

Creative disruption is at its most extreme when a physical product goes digital, experiencing the shift described by Nicholas Negroponte in his 1993 classic *Being Digital* from 'atoms to bytes'. Once this happens, the whole industry finds itself having to adapt to this new physics of business with often violent consequences. This is what has happened to music, news, classified advertising, directories, encyclopaedias, movies and photography: a radical disruption in the economics of both creation and distribution.

These businesses all face the twin challenges of sustaining a traditional business and its accompanying infrastructure as it goes into a state of terminal decline, while at the same time having to invest in developing a new business with completely different economics, requiring very different skills and operating in a completely different competitive landscape. It is here that the greatest risk lies to traditional businesses, and the most radical action has to be taken as a result.

2 Digital products face digital distribution

The second level of disruption is for 'digital products' such as software and computer games that have traditionally been tied to physical forms of distribution. The creators and retailers of these products face disruption sometimes from being distributed digitally and sometimes from being hosted 'in the cloud'. Rather than being downloaded or installed, they are accessed over the internet via a web browser. In the enterprise software market, this is where Salesforce.com led the way, changing the nature of CRM software from something that required major installation and access over an internal network to something that anyone in the company could instantly access from any internet connected computer.

The single biggest battle being fought in 2010 is with Microsoft Office – a disc-based product – facing a sustained attack from the development of Google Apps – a cloud-based product that offers reduced functionality but at an even more reduced price. (For a business, a move to Google Apps can reduce costs by 80–90%.)

With computer games there is a similar looming disruption with the shift from buying discs to downloading games straight to an Xbox, PlayStation or Wii. This could potentially disintermediate both high street and online retailers (something which they are resisting furiously). Threats also come from the development of hosted games on Facebook and other social networks. In both cases, there is a shift in the economic model: from one-off payments to subscriptions or to a 'freemium' model such as that employed by many Facebook games where it is free to start playing or using the software, but you pay for extras.

There is also a shift in the creative process: physical distribution means fewer bigger releases to take the product forward; hosted software and games are continuously tweaked. The mantras of web-based software – 'release early and often' – and the idea of 'perpetual beta' are a complete anathema to the world of physically distributed software.

3 Physical and invisible products

The third degree is in the world of products that can't be digitised or that were invisible anyway – such as travel, financial services or clothing. Here the product and its pricing structure remains, but there is a disruption in the chain of transactions between producer and consumer. Increased efficiency here leads to lower prices, so we find *cheaper* books, flights and jeans, but we can't download them for free. The most obvious potential threat is disintermediation as retailers and agents find themselves cut out. This has been a factor in some sectors: in Chapter 7, I describe how British Airways used the internet to disintermediate intermediaries, improve its relationship with its consumers, and save £100m a year in the process.

This is a real phenomenon in many sectors and, as I'll discuss later, in the coming years it will become even more so, but a much bigger trend has been the evolution of new intermediaries. They offer previously impossible services to consumers, be it the price comparison offered by MoneySupermarket, the infinite shelves of Amazon, or the ability to watch programmes from News Corp, NBC and Disney whenever you want on Hulu. And thanks to the new physics of business, they can do it all from a much lower cost base, challenging those who held the intermediary positions beforehand.

For the creators of these goods there is one massive threat: the development of new, near dominant intermediaries. Amazon has achieved this in the world of book publishing and secured phenomenal negotiating power over publishers as a result.

The challenge for traditional intermediaries, be they travel agents, financial advisers, estate agents or clothing retailers, is still one of reinvention. Those who once simply acted as gatekeepers because there was no alternative for consumers now have to compete in a new world, securing whatever competitive advantage they can from their traditional strengths: usually a mix of brand, physical presence, as well as their

> ❝ the challenge for traditional intermediaries is still one of reinvention ❞

buying power with suppliers and their relationship with consumers. Traditional retailers who not only develop websites but also offer 'click and collect' services are doing exactly this. So too are travel agents, who carefully manage a mix of channels – web, call centre and physical retail – across a single brand.

Of these three degrees of disruption, the first of these is the most consistently challenging. For the second and third much more depends on the external factors we discuss in the next chapter, and on some of the characteristics that are vital for successful reinvention, as discussed in Chapter 4.

The fortunate few: those who shall not be disrupted

Creators of non-commodity products that cannot be digitised have the sudden potential to reach a global audience: the internet provides a shop window they never had. This might be a widget manufacturer in Michigan, a jeweller in Jaipur, a creator of luxurious stationery in Hamburg or a children's entertainer in Aberdeen. All have new routes to market thanks to the online world. The media or other intermediaries that they once might have used to find customers will suffer, but for them, there is only opportunity.

Service businesses, from management consultants and lawyers to advertising and marketing agencies and headhunters, are also structurally safe because ultimately the core of their job involves their clients employing them to do something that they can't do themselves, and can't get a piece of software to do it for them. This doesn't mean that their lives are getting any easier. They need to develop or buy in new capabilities to reinvent their role for the digital age, and there will be many who fall by the wayside as a result of not doing so. An ad agency that doesn't have a good grasp of digital creativity and execution, a PR consultancy that doesn't know how to protect its clients' reputations on social networks, or a big consultancy that can't advise clients on how to develop a digital strategy, all have limited shelf lives. But this is about competition and competence, rather than their industries suddenly becoming structurally disadvantaged.

For some businesses, their sources of competitive advantage are so embedded in the physical world that they remain intact throughout the market's move online. Supermarkets are a good example. Even if you put up a competing website, businesses such as Tesco, Wal-Mart or LeClerc operate at such a scale, and require so much in the way of physical logistics and buying power to bring in a vast range of goods and then get them out to customers. Add to this the power of their brands and it is clear that the internet is just another channel to which they can bring all their advantages. Their economic moats, in other words, stay intact, and it is ferociously difficult to compete with them head on. Ocado in the UK has proved that it is possible to create a national online-only supermarket, but this is a niche addition to the pack rather than a structural challenge to any of the major chains.

Similarly, a distinctive retailer such as Philip Green's Top Shop still has scarcity in its offer of cheap, high fashion clothing. As long as they continue to deliver on their core promise as a business, the internet simply allows them to reach even more customers with greater efficiency.

❝ there is one clear area of potential value creation ❞

Finally, even in the maelstrom of content businesses that have to go from print to digital, there is one clear area of potential value creation – and that is in the world of highly specialised professional information and data. This is the world of Thomson Reuters, Reed Elsevier and others. Here the internet has enabled the potential to provide an infinitely superior service for customers and, importantly, charge more for it as a result. Fat books of legal cases become searchable databases available to anyone in a subscribing company wherever they have access to the internet (which increasingly will mean on their smartphones as well). A dusty journal of radiology can become a workflow console that sits alongside an x-ray terminal, allowing a radiographer to check exactly what he's looking at without having to go to the shelves and manually flick through indexes.

External forces of creative disruption

The internet might create a new physics of business, and some businesses and industries might be particularly vulnerable to that, but the real extent of creative disruption depends on a combination of four interdependent external forces. Two of these forces are very human, one is technological, and the final one is purely financial. And they all have one defining characteristic: as an incumbent, you can't do anything about them. They are:

- entrepreneurs and new entrants
- what people want and need
- device proliferation
- economic volatility.

As we look back over the period since 1993, it becomes clear that the more these four forces are at play in your market, the greater the challenges you will face. The reason it is clear to me that this era of creative disruption still has years to run is that these four forces are not going to go away. In fact, we can predict they are only going to become more prevalent in most markets over the next decade.

New entrants and entrepreneurs

One of the characteristics that differentiated Schumpeter's thinking from economists who had gone before him, and one of the reasons why I became such a fan of his work, was the emphasis he placed on entrepreneurs – 'new men' and 'new businesses' as he called them – to drive profound change. These were more than inventors, these were the people who seized the technological advances and used them to transform our world. It is the difference between Sir Tim Berners Lee – who invented the world wide web – and Jeff Bezos, who then built on that invention to change the way the world shops and in doing so created $50bn of shareholder value.

Incumbent businesses enjoying strong profits in their sectors have no incentive to disrupt their own world – even when they know the

⁶⁶ think of how Google has changed the world of media ⁹⁹ technology exists to do so. It is almost always left to outsiders: both entrepreneurial start-ups or big businesses invading adjacent markets. Think of how Google has changed the world of media, advertising and now software; and think of Apple's impact on both the music and mobile phone industries. Google was the ultimate start-up, Apple a multi-billion dollar corporation looking for new growth areas: both have profoundly upset 'the way of doing things' in sectors in a way that no incumbent would ever have been willing to do. Skype is a great example of this. No telecom incumbent would have launched the service – it is far too damaging to their traditional model. The labs at British Telecom or Verizon might have been able to deliver a similar product – but they would have deemed it commercial suicide to deliver it.

Since 1993, a relatively small set of individuals and organisations have brought about spectacular change throughout the business world. If you look at Table 2.1, you can see just how much change has been sparked by the creations of just 25 entrepreneurs.

Table 2.1 Twenty five entrepreneurs and their creations

Entrepreneurs	Company	Achievement	Profitable?	Financial scale
Tony Hsieh	Zappos	Defied retail logic by getting people to buy shoes online	Yes	Sold to Amazon for $900m in 2009
Brent Hoberman and Martha Lane Fox	LastMinute.com	Created a new proposition in the travel industry and one of Europe's great e-commerce success stories	Yes	Sold to Sabre for $1.1bn in 2005
Larry Page and Sergey Brin	Google	Changed the way the world of information and commerce operated	Yes	Market cap £150bn by June 2010
Mark Zuckerberg	Facebook	450m users signed up to the world's leading social network	Yes	Valued at $10bn in 2009
Natalie Massenet	Net-a-Porter	Defied conventional wisdom with its success of a high-end fashion store	Yes	Sold to Richemont at a value of £350m in 2010

▶

Entrepreneurs	Company	Achievement	Profitable?	Financial scale
Jeff Bezos	Amazon	Reinvented book retailing; expanded across the e-commerce spectrum	Yes	Market cap in March 2010: 55bn
Andrew Black and Edward Wray	Betfair	Developed a completely new form of betting where people bet against each other rather than the bookmaker	Yes	2009: £79m EBITDA on £303m revenue
Niklas Zennstrom, Janus Friis	Skype	Reduced the price of international voice and video calls to zero	Yes	Sold in 2009 for $2.75bn
Chad Hurley, Steve Chen, Jawed Karim	YouTube	Made the creation, distribution and consumption of video on the internet a mass market phenomenon	No	Sold to Google for $1.65bn
Dave Filo, Jerry Yang	Yahoo!	Created the idea of the 'portal', taming the internet for the first wave of internet users	Yes	Market cap $22bn
Mark Benioff	Salesforce.com	Redefined the nature of enterprise software by offering hosted CRM solutions	Yes	Market cap in March 2010: $8.7bn
Reed Hastings	Netflix	Redefined the movie rental business	Yes	Market Cap in March 2010: $3.6bn
Craig Newmark	Craigslist	Transformed the world of classified advertising	Yes	$100m revenues (est.) in 2009
Jeff Taylor	Monster	Built an international recruitment service challenging print publications of every kind	Yes	$2bn market cap
Reid Hoffman	LinkedIn	Developed a global professional networking site unlike anything that has existed before: a vital part of the professional recruitment value chain	Yes	Estimated valuation $1bn
Elon Musk	Paypal	Enabled simple and secure transactions over the internet with a smarter solution than anything offered by any bank	Yes	Sold to eBay for $1.5bn
Simon Nixon	Money Supermarket	Empowered consumers with price comparisons of financial and travel products	Yes	$500m market cap
Pierre Omidyar	eBay	Allowed anyone to sell (pretty much) anything to anyone	Yes	$30bn market cap

This isn't a definitive list of big internet businesses – there have been many more that have been bought and sold for hundreds of millions – but from this collection alone, in a period of little more than 15 years, 25 people have created profitable businesses with an asset value of about $130bn. And that is before you add in Google, where two more people (helped by CEO Eric Schmidt) sit in pole position with a market cap of around $150bn.

In each case these entrepreneurs have changed the way that people have had to think about their sector, or created businesses that simply could not have existed before, as is the case with Facebook and Google. All of the businesses above succeeded because they created something that people love to use – not just because of the concept, but because of the execution.

This is why it is dangerous just to think of entrepreneurs throughout this period as 'disruptors'. As Niklas Zennstrom, one of the founders of Skype describes it:

It's not about what you destroy it's what you create. It's about seizing changes in technology, regulatory changes, and changes in how consumers are behaving, so you can do something much more efficiently – do it in a completely different way.[3]

So entrepreneurs are a critical force, creating products and services that change markets, and when they get it right, creating significant value along the way. Yes, there will always be over-valued and hyped businesses and investment bubbles, but for those who get it right, the rewards are spectacular.

There are two more important characteristics in the way that entre-preneurs redefine and disrupt markets. First, they will often succeed by defying conventional wisdom. Natalie Massenet built a formidable global retail business with Net-a-Porter, selling high-value designer clothing over the internet. It was conventional wisdom that women

---

3 Speaking on stage at DLD in Hamburg, February 2010.

would only ever want to buy this kind of clothing in a store, after trying it on and enjoying the physical retail experience. In fact, a mix of great service and formidable online execution has allowed the company to blow holes in accepted wisdom. The same is true of Tony Hsieh's Zappos, which has succeeded in selling shoes online when everyone in the industry believed no-one would buy shoes without being able to try them on first (Zappos instead made it easy for people to order three sizes and then send the ones that didn't fit back.) And, as the box below demonstrates, Reed Hastings has built a formidable business by defying the perceived wisdom that the future of video rental was all about downloads and instead offering a mail order subscription service for DVDs.

Netflix: and the entrepreneur's knack of defying conventional wisdom

If you had gone to business school in 1998 and discussed the future of the video market, you would have been told one thing: it was going to be about downloads and video on demand. That was the future according to anyone who knew about these things.

Reed Hastings, however, had another idea. He found himself paying a \$40 fee for bringing a copy of *Apollo 13* back to Blockbuster six weeks late. He faced a dilemma: should he tell his wife about the fine and face the inevitable scorn and derision, or should he just lie and say they let him off.

Hastings realised something was wrong with a business that put him in this position: 'I'm thinking about lying to my wife about a late fee and the sanctity of my marriage for this thing! I mean it was just crazy. And I was on the way to the gym and I realised – "Whoa! Video stores could operate like a gym, with a flat membership fee." And it was like "I wonder why no one's done that before!"'[4]

In 1998, Hastings launched an online DVD rental business, based on a subscription fee, with a simple promise: 'no late fees'. You set

4 CBS News, *The Brain behind Netflix,* 3 December 2006, www.cbsnews.com/stories/2006/12/01/60minutes/main2222059.shtml

up your queue of DVDs online and they appear in the post. When you've seen a DVD you send it back for free and the next disc in your list is sent out to you. That business, of course, is Netflix. It now sends out around half a billion DVDs each year to millions of customers, and in 2009 its revenues stood at $1.7 bn with a market capitalisation (in July 2010) of more than $5bn.

The film market will move to downloads and online streaming and Netflix – and its European equivalent LOVEFiLM – already offer digital download services. Whenever interviewed, Hastings talks openly about having to transition the business to a digital future. But even in 2010, 12 years after launching, he can now do that on the back of a strong, cash-generating, core business.

Interestingly, Blockbuster had the chance to buy Netflix before it was profitable for $50m. They turned it down and instead decided they would by-pass the awkward business of posting out DVDs and go straight to downloads instead. So in 2000 Blockbuster signed up for a 20-year exclusive deal with a dynamic provider of broadband services to deliver movies digitally to people's homes. And the company they signed with? It was called Enron. The project never got past the test stage and it all ended acrimoniously.[5]

The other characteristic of entrepreneurs in the digital age is that once they start in a sector, they never stop. The first wave of start-ups disrupt physical businesses, but as these digital pioneers get entrenched, they face disruption from the next wave who offer something that changes the rules yet again.

In the travel world, for example, Expedia and Travelocity took the market by storm in the first wave. They benefited from having much lower costs than traditional travel agents and consumers benefited from lower prices and new levels of convenience as a result. Brent Hoberman and Martha Lane-Fox's Lastminute.com added a further

5 Despite the utter failure of the Blockbuster–Enron deal in generating any consumer business, Enron's creative accounting still meant it generated £111m in revenue according to Forbes, www.forbes.com/2003/03/13/cx_da_0313topnews.html

twist by specialising in remnant inventory from hotels and airlines – and became, for better and worse, an icon of the dotcom boom in the UK before selling up to Travelocity for $1.1bn.

But, more recently, this first wave of online travel agents, have faced disruption themselves. In 2001, three IT professionals who found it difficult trying to work out which cut-price airline flight to choose when they were heading off for a skiing holiday, developed SkyScanner which aggregated all the flight prices and times from all of the budget airlines, and in doing so created a new type of travel intermediary.

The same model was adopted and developed on a global scale in 2004 when three veterans of the online travel world (if it is possible to have 'veterans' in an industry that is less than a decade old) launched Kayak.com, which again reinvented the intermediary role in travel with a vertical search engine. They don't act as agents in a traditional sense – they aggregate data from airlines and online travel agents, and get paid for referrals. Kayak is both a driver of business to Expedia and its like, and a competitor. No doubt someone, somewhere, is working on an even smarter way to help people find the flights and hotels that they want and will build a $100m business on the back of it. This is what entrepreneurs do – and their relentless pursuit of the next big idea is one of the reasons why the era of creative disruption still has many years to run.

❝ the era of creative disruption still has many years to run ❞

What people want and need

While the internet can make a host of things possible and entrepreneurs can then seize upon those possibilities, it is only when this actually ties in with what people want and need that the magic (or as some might see it, the mayhem) starts to happen.

The internet has not, I believe, fundamentally changed what we want and need. But it has exponentially transformed how some of those wants and needs can be satisfied. And once someone has given you exactly what you want – it's very difficult to settle for anything less.

There are four broad areas of desire that the internet has enabled to be satisfied. Invariably it is when smart entrepreneurs create products and services that allow one or more of these wants and needs to be satisfied, that they strike gold; and those who have traditionally made a living from businesses that don't meet these needs as well can expect to find themselves severely challenged.

1 We want to create, communicate and connect

Mankind has been creative since cave paintings. We have adopted every technology possible to improve communication. And institution after institution – social, professional and political – is based on our desire to connect with people like us.

The internet has brought all of this together under one umbrella of activity. Creativity used to be much more of a solitary act – something done in isolation until your work was finished, at which point it was shared one-to-one, or hopefully gained the endorsement of a media outlet to reach a wider audience.

In the online world, creativity has become the start of a shared, social experience. You upload your photos to Flickr. You write on a blog and tell people about it on Twitter. You post your videos to YouTube. You make music and share it on MySpace.

Even when we are at our most passive – consuming reality TV or movie blockbusters – we then use the internet to turn this into a shared experience, following a stream of tweets, joining a Facebook group, or checking the Wikipedia page about what we have just watched and correcting any mistakes.

And, the benefit of the internet is that our potential to connect is unlike anything we have ever known before. Our school and college friends are never more than a Facebook message away. No matter what we are interested in, be it cross-stitching, karaoke or taxidermy, it is always possible to find someone else who is interested in it as well.

2 We want to challenge authority

After Simon Cowell had dominated the Christmas charts for four years running, and a perfectly innocent teenager called Joe Mceldrey had won the *X-factor* (the equivalent of *Pop Idol*) in December 2009, it seemed certain that there would be a fifth successive victory for one of Cowell's protégés. However, a couple called Tracy and John Moter had different plans. They started a Facebook group, encouraging people to buy 'Killing In The Name' by the rap-metal group Rage Against the Machine and make it the Christmas number one instead. Within a week there were nearly a million people as part of the group. The media covered the story, further stoking the fire. When it came to Christmas, Rage Against the Machine was number one and the stranglehold on the Christmas number one slot was suddenly broken.

What was remarkable about the whole phenomenon was how easy it was. To achieve his dominance for the past four years, Cowell and the broadcaster ITV had had to conceive some of the most successful formats in television history, deliver staggering audiences, and then flood the retail market. You might not like the result, but they had fine tuned the machine to deliver results way ahead of anything achieved before. No traditional music operation had come anywhere near that success, but it was all unravelled by a Facebook group.

Since the internet became a mainstream phenomenon, it has provided the perfect outlet for people who want to vent, rant and take some form of action against the powers that be. This energy and frustration existed before, but the desire to do something about it can now be exponentially satisfied. And much of the excitement about Web 2.0 came from examples of 'the crowd giving it to the man': be it bloggers bringing down Dan Rather by revealing flaws in a CBS report claiming

George W. Bush dodged the draft; or British students protesting on Facebook about HSBC putting its bank charges up, thus forcing a U-turn from the bank. Since David slayed Goliath we have loved this kind of story, and the internet allows it to happen with greater frequency and severity than any technological advance before it.

For entrepreneurs, too, this is a rich seam to mine – allowing them to build businesses that position themselves as challengers to tired, traditional incumbents. The collective wisdom of Wikipedia gets pitched against the top-down hierarchy of Britannica. Skype is the antithesis of a traditional telco, liberating you from your phone bill. Bloggers rail against the mainstream media. Craigslist is the antithesis of expensive, boring newspaper classified businesses. The pitch is that these businesses are on *your* side and, in most cases, the pitch is absolutely true.

❝ bloggers rail against the mainstream media ❞

My particular favourite is the way that Mark Benioff, founder and CEO of Salesforce.com, wastes no opportunity to kick against the big incumbents in enterprise software, namely Microsoft, Oracle and SAP. In an internal e-mail he described SAP as an 'innovation-free company'[6] adding 'their code is as bulky and inefficient as it is expensive and unloved by its users'. Faced with a rival hosted product from Microsoft in 1997, he said: 'Microsoft's strategy of an inferior product at an inferior price promises to do for on-demand what Zune [Microsoft's struggling iPod-wannabe] has done for music players.'[7] Of Oracle he said their 'killer app is acquisitions ... You have to give Larry (Ellison, the CEO) credit for the ability to ingest companies and spit out their numbers'.[8]

To define Salesforce, Wikipedia or any of these organisations by what they're not does them a great disservice. Ultimately they all succeed

6 www.businessweek.com/the_thread/techbeat/archives/2006/02/sap_vs_salesfor.html
7 www.theregister.co.uk/2007/08/16/salesforce_second_quarter_sap/
8 Ibid.

by offering brilliant products and services for consumers. But part of what makes them fly is the fact that like the idea of taking Rage Against the Machine to Christmas number one, they tap into our deep desire to see the powers that be challenged – and ideally to play some role in that.

3   We want bargains and freebies

There is nothing new about 'free' or our desire for freebies. Z. John Zhang, a Wharton marketing professor who has authored books on pricing strategy, says that 'Free' has been around 'probably since the beginning of business'. 'Free', he says, 'is one of the most powerful words in marketing. It truly motivates people. If you see "free," even if you don't want it, you're going to get it. Marketers will take every opportunity to use that word.'[9]

The phrase 'information wants to be free' has been one of the mantras of the internet, but it is, frankly, a nonsense. Information can't *want* anything. That is just a geekish anthropomorphism. *People* want information to be free, and on the internet there is normally someone who is going to provide it for them.

The undeniable attraction of the internet for many people, especially later adopters, is that you can get things that you previously had to pay for without having to pay for them, including newspapers, music and content of every kind. Rupert Murdoch has decided this can't go on, and has put pay walls around *The Times* and *Sunday Times* in the UK. I know from personal experience it is fiendishly difficult to have a financially successful newspaper website without anyone paying to access your content. But, I suspect he will find it is even harder to do so by charging when everyone else isn't.

As we have also seen, the economics of running online retailers and intermediaries – with no need for the fixed costs of those who have traditionally operated here in these areas – has also meant a flood

9 Quoted in 'How About Free?' *Knowledge@Wharton*, March 2009, http://bit.ly/16iZyb

of bargains. 'Internet prices' has become synonymous with 'massive discounts'. When we go online we expect to find cheap flights, cheap DVDs and cheap TVs.

As we'll see when discussing the importance of economic cycles later, the internet's reputation for bargains and freebies is a fundamental factor in its growth, and in the disruption it has caused. We have just got used to things being cheaper or free and this means that those who operate in the physical world have to compete, either by justifying their premium to us through choice, convenience or true distinctiveness, or more often by changing their economics so they can survive on internet prices.

4 We want our lives to be easier

We live in chaotic and fragmented times. We have never had so much choice of products and so much information thrown at us. We will move homes and jobs more than our parents and grandparents ever did. We will visit more countries than them, and eat and drink in hundreds more places. With every decision we have to make, there is more and more information supposedly to help us make it. We look at old age with unprecedented uncertainty about when we might be able to retire and what we will have to live on.

Consequently, in both our professional and personal lives we seek out suppliers of products and services that make us feel better equipped to deal with the world, and make life easier for us. Successful businesses help us get what we want, where we want it – and to echo Niklas Zennstrom's words above, allow us to do it with an efficiency that was previously inconceivable.

There are four ways that the internet has made our lives easier:

■ **Aggregation**: Google News, Money Supermarket and Kayak are just three examples of services that bring together a vast collection of sources in a single place, making them easy for us to access in our own time. This is a formidable consumer benefit.

- **Time-shifting**: the capability to do things when and where we want has been spectacularly liberating. Being able to check your bank balance any time of day or night; place a supermarket order while having a glass of wine in the evening; or watch last night's TV tonight – these are all quantum leaps in convenience from the way we lived even 15 years ago.
- **Personalisation**: on a whole host of levels we can make things our own. We can craft our own cocktails of news and information using Netvibes or iGoogle. We can have a radio station based on the music we like at Last.fm or Pandora. Our retail experiences can be based on things we have previously bought or looked at.
- **Immediacy**: the gaps between events happening and people finding out about them are continuously shrinking. So too is the gap between any desire (of the consumer kind!) being aroused and satisfied. The second someone recommends a book to you, you can download it on your Kindle. You can see someone wearing a jacket in a magazine at 9 a.m., and have it ordered and on its way to you by 9.05 a.m.

There is money in making life easier for people – in fact it is the best way to counter the expectation of 'internet prices'. I shop at Ocado rather than Tesco.com because they deliver within a one-hour window rather than a two-hour window – but I pay more as a result. I sign up to Amazon Prime because I know I can just press a button and my order will be with me within 24 hours, which means I don't check the prices from other retailers.

When we launched the first Guardian iPhone App we were also the first UK newspaper to charge for an application like this. We felt confident doing so because we added a host of features, such as offline reading, to make it easier for people to get what they wanted when they wanted. We sold 100,000 within the first three months – far outstripping our – and everyone else's – expectations.

There is going to be even greater levels of convenience and immediacy in our world in the coming years as the mobile internet starts to grow dramatically. Which brings us neatly to our next force of disruption.

Device proliferation

The more connected devices there are in the world, the more time and money we spend online – and so the potential for creative disruption increases.

The period since the collapse of the dotcom bubble has seen the internet move away from the fixed desktop. Laptops with Wi-Fi are the norm and it is completely natural for families to sit down in the evening in front of the TV, each with a laptop on their knees as they shop, click through Facebook, send e-mails, look up holiday destinations or, if they are particularly anti-social, watch a completely different TV programme to the one everyone else has in front of them. This is not an insignificant phenomenon.

❝ this is not an insignificant phenomenon ❞

It is something that tens of millions of people do every night, and this development of a whole new type of internet consumption helped to contribute to the dramatic upturn in the online economy. There are now about one billion PCs and laptops in the world. The number is unlikely to increase dramatically in the coming years but the number of internet-connected devices is, thanks to the the ever-growing market in mobile devices.

In December 2009, the analysts at Morgan Stanley put out a hefty report on the mobile internet. Figure 2.1 overleaf shows an (approximate) logarithmic increase in the number of devices with each wave of computing. The analysts concluded that: 'The mobile internet has the potential to create/destroy more wealth than prior computer cycles … more users will likely connect to the internet via mobile than desktop within 5 years.'[10]

This is why in 2010 we have Amazon, Google and Apple all jostling for space in the mobile market. They know that mobile means growth, and as the number of PCs starts to plateau, growth is increasingly

10 Morgan Stanley, *Mobile Internet Report*, December 2009.

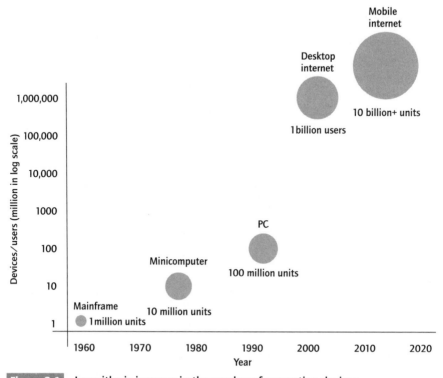

Source: Adapted from Morgan Stanley, *Mobile Internet Report*, December 2009

Figure 2.1 Logarithmic increase in the number of computing devices

going to come from mobile platforms. Whether these devices are smartphones as we know them, iterations of Apple's iPad or Amazon's Kindle or souped-up versions of any of the countless e-readers that arrived onto the market in 2010 is not important. The simple fact is that these billions of powerful connected devices in people's hands driving another change in consumer behaviour.

Anyone who owns an iPhone knows that simply having a richly featured device with you at all times that is a pleasure to use, dramatically increases your access to a whole range of internet services and applications. You check train times as you're waiting at the station on your mobile. You check news headlines when you're sitting in Starbucks, or post a picture to Twitter when you're waiting for a bus. In order to keep your children quiet in a traffic jam, you let them watch pictures of sneezing pandas on YouTube (yes, I speak from personal experience on that one). These are all relatively trivial acts, but as with the example of families watching TV with their individual laptops, when they're carried out by hundreds of millions of people around the world they bring massive opportunities, but also spectacular threats for businesses that have no meaningful mobile presence.

Economic volatility

We have been on something of an economic rollercoaster since the launch of Mosaic in 1993. We have experienced one spectacular investment bubble, and a consequent crash. We went through one of most sustained periods of economic growth in living memory – and then one of the deepest recessions. We also squeezed in a global economic slowdown after 9/11, the collapse of Lehmans and the subsequent squeeze on credit markets. If you read many descriptions of how the internet has affected traditional businesses, it is often as if all of this hadn't happened. People talk about technology and consumers. But, the truth is that this particularly volatile couple of decades in the global economy has been critical in the process of creative disruption.

One impact is a general one. Economic volatility, whether up or down, dictates the day-to-day agenda in most businesses. A boom leaves everyone chasing growth at all cost, and often clouds judgement about risk. A downturn makes everyone spectacularly short sighted. Nothing matters except trying to fix the business *now*: sorting out the future is not an immediate priority.

The consequence is that when you have had nearly two decades where the economy has consistently seemed to be either very good, or very bad, the moments for clear-headed judgement and cool deliberation are few and far between, especially when you are having to answer to shareholders on a quarterly basis. And yet, if ever there has been a time to take a objective look at your organisation's strengths and weaknesses, or to fundamentally challenge your assumptions about your customers, your consumers and your competitors – it has been now and in the past decade.

There have been three specific phenomena as a result of the volatility we have experienced since 1993.

1   The dotcom bust fooled everyone

When the Nasdaq crashed in 2000/01, and a wave of dotcom start-ups went to the wall, the general reaction in many incumbent businesses was that the internet had been and gone and left them intact. Internet investments were frozen and sites were run on skeletal staff. Newspaper and directory businesses took on debt to buy each other up, and retailers let Amazon carry on piling up losses, confident that the internet would only ever be a niche phenomenon.

Meanwhile, broadband penetration was rising, blogging was moving into the mainstream and a company called Google was starting to make a profit thanks to its rather clever automated advertising platform. And every year consumers spent more time and money online. When it became clear that this was not going to go away, many businesses found themselves fighting hard to catch up. It took until 2005 for Rupert Murdoch, for example, to show any enthusiasm for the internet. Many of the traditional media organisations generally deemed to have done best on the internet all continued to invest during this period including Schibsted in Norway, Naspers in South Africa, the BBC and (if I may say so myself) the *Guardian* in the UK.

2   Downturns have accelerated structural change

In the two significant downturns since 1993 – the slowdown after 9/11 and the 2008/09 recession – there was much debate among disrupted businesses about what is 'structural decline' and what is 'cyclical'. For CEOs speaking to investors it was standard practice to put any poor performance down to purely cyclical factors – because the alternative was too horrific for them or their shareholders to contemplate.

The truth appears to have been more brutal: cyclical downturns have consistently accelerated structural change, a result of both businesses and consumers turning to the internet to save money. This has been particularly prevalent in travel. Lastminute.com for example experienced strong revenue growth after 9/11, while in the final quarter of 2009, Priceline – by now a relatively mature business – sold 44% more airline tickets than it had done the year before. This was a spectacular result given that volumes for the period were down by 9% in the market.[11]

❝ the impact has been brutal on newspaper recruitment advertising ❞

The impact has been brutal on newspaper recruitment advertising, which has always been a cyclical business. In both downturns, the shift away from print accelerated as businesses looked to reduce their spend in the short term. When they started spending again, it was increasingly on the internet. They had found that it worked, and it was cheaper: what's not to like?

Meanwhile Google has been a consistent beneficiary of this structural shift. Its advertising business succeeded through the 2008/09 recession because it is based on response, and therefore is less risky for advertisers. And as more retail expenditure has shifted online, so more retailer advertising has gone Google's way.

Meanwhile Google Apps' business has emerged as a way to save a significant amount of money on your e-mail system. A few years earlier, this might have been deemed an operational risk, but it is now music to the ear of any chief executive desperately trying to reduce cost. It is, of course, spectacularly bad news for Microsoft as they see the first evidence of disruption to their Office business.

3 The credit crunch squeezed debt-laden incumbents

After the collapse of Lehmans, the debt markets completely froze up, and with this came a new set of troubles to many incumbent businesses facing disruption. First, it took private equity purchasers out of the

---

11 http://www.axses.com/encyc/archive/arcres/arcrates/users2/news09/expedia-priceline-inrecession.htm

market. A wave of debt-laden private equity purchases had kept many traditional media stock prices high, but when these buyers were taken out of the market and the recession started to bite share prices went into freefall. Many businesses had also taken on significant debt – often in acquisition sprees after the dotcom bubble had burst. Their priority had been consolidation and margin growth, but as the economy slowed down they found themselves in danger of breaching the covenants on those debts and potentially being taken over by their banks.

The phenomenon was widespread – I lived through it on the board of the Nordics directory business Eniro. Restructuring debt dominates boardrooms for months on end. It makes the need to conserve cash even more extreme and so in many cases yet again dampened the potential for meaningful internet investment. The result is that strategic options are whittled away at the very time when they need to be opened up. At Eniro, the conclusion was a successful rights issue and a dramatic reduction in debt levels as a result – but others are often not so lucky. In particular, for some private equity owned businesses the consequences were even more pronounced, as we discuss in Chapter 4 with particular reference to Terra Firma's takeover of EMI.

My suspicion is that the next wave of economic growth, coming after 2012, is going to deliver another twist in this tale. It will be at this point that the 'cyclical' recovery many disrupted businesses have predicted will fail to appear, and those who have failed to build substantial internet businesses will find it difficult to achieve any meaningful level of growth. This takes us to the next wave of creative disruption.

Creative disruption – bad news for porn stars

In the early days of the internet, pornography seemed to be the one form of content that you could make money from. While sites in pretty much every other corner of the media and entertainment industry gave their content away for free, porn sites could charge. But the party soon came to an end.

'Everyone was excited because they thought the internet was going to affect our business in a positive way, and it's been the opposite … it's been a little scary,'[12] according to David Joseph the founder of adult video producers Red Light District.

The problem has been a typical weakening of the incumbents' position in the face of creative disruption. Barriers to entry dropped – first with hundreds of entrepreneurs setting up adult sites and driving subscription prices down, then came a whole host of free porn sites based on YouTube, such as Red Tube and Porn Tube: these attracted millions of users, but sucked value out of the market.

As broadband spread, the DVD market went into freefall. Paul Fishbein of the industry trade magazine, *Adult Video News*, estimated that it fell in the US by some 50% or around $1.8bn between 2006 and 2009.[13] Internet revenues simply weren't making up for this drop. By early in 2009, Playboy, which was a third smaller than it had been in 2005, announced the company was pulling out of the DVD market all together.

This has meant changing times for porn stars. Few businesses will now make features, instead they focus on short episodes for online sites and mobile phones – where the figleaf of a plot has now been completely removed.

One porn star, Savanna Samson, recalls the difference between the roles she used to have, and those she was getting now: 'I used to have dialogue,' she said, bemoaning the fact that 'getting it on in one hardcore scene after another just isn't as much fun'.[14]

According to another of the industry's big names, Jesse Jane, the real money comes from the one medium where she can still create scarcity – live performance: 'I do six films a year, but I make much more from appearing live. I don't dance a lot, I pick seven or eight venues a year, and if you're not doing a lot, people want you even more at their club because it is exclusive.'[15]

---

12 'Obscene Losses', *Portfolio*, November 2007.
13 'Lights, Camera, Lots of Action, Forget The Script', *New York Times*, 7 July, 2009.
14 Ibid.
15 Interviewed in 'The Business of Pleasure', *CNBC*, 17 July 2009.

The next wave of creative disruption

All of the factors discussed on the previous pages are still with us, and they are not going to go away. In fact, the growth of the mobile internet, the return of economic growth after 2012, and the constant potential for entrepreneurs to come up with products and services that satisfy fundamental consumer need are, I believe, going to drive another great wave of creative disruption in the near future.

In the epilogue to this book, I take a hesitant look into the future – an exercise that is always dangerous. But for now, it is enough to look at where some of the flashpoints might be. As you start to consider some of the questions below, it becomes clear that the potential for both creation and disruption in the years ahead is just as great, if not greater, than it has been for the past 15 years.

- The generation that was just starting school when Marc Andreessen launched Netscape will no longer be digital consumers, but business leaders and decision makers. What tools will they expect their staff to use? What level of information will they expect about their customers? What marketing strategies will they adopt?
- Google is currently working on live translation technology. Imagine a world where any content or conversation that is passed over the internet could be translated into any language and back in real time. What potential for business, politics or education would that throw open?
- What will happen inside our homes when we have super-fast broadband and internet-connected televisions as the norm?
- The movie business, book publishing and computer games are still predominately distributed physically. CDs still account for 80% of the value in the music market. What will be the impact of these markets going digital – both for those who create them and for the retailers who sell them?
- US newspaper revenues – including the internet – stood at $37bn in 2008, down from a peak of $48bn in 2000. What will the

industry look like if that figure drops by another \$10–\$15bn over the next ten years?

■ Even the travel sector in the US, one of the first to go digital, is still less than 50% online. What will be the economics of the global travel market when it is 70–80% online?

■ The economics of the movie and TV industries is still based around release windows for different formats, different channels and different regions. How long will this be sustainable? What will be the impact?

■ The majority of phone calls are still made over fixed lines or GSM networks rather than over internet protocol. Skype is a \$500m business and Verizon a \$100bn business – what will those numbers be in a decade's time?

■ What will YouTube morph into over the next decade? We can already see it moving to serve full versions of TV shows and potentially paid-for movies. It aims to be the global default for watching video on the PC or mobile. Will it have the same dominance in the living room in ten years' time?

■ Only a small percentage of India's one billion population is currently online. What will be the impact of hundreds of millions of Indian consumers going online entirely via their mobile phones?

■ Where will the hype about 'cloud computing' take us? What applications will a major organisation actually host and what impact will this have on the likes of Oracle, SAP and Microsoft? What software will the average office employee in a US company sit down in front of every day in 2023?

■ What will happen to the world's postal services – all massive employers – if we are posting 80% less letters in ten years' time than we are now?

■ Internet advertising still accounts for less than 10% globally. Martin Sorrell, the chief executive of WPP, believes that figure will rise to something closer to the proportion of people's time spent online – 20%. What will that mean for other media?

■ Packaged goods manufacturers all still sell through major retailers who also compete with them by offering their own branded goods. When will they start to sell direct? Procter and Gamble announced a small trial in 2009 and has taken a stake in Ocado. Where will this lead?

We can speculate for hours about the answers to each of these questions, but if the last 15 years of creative disruption have taught us anything, it is that we might have some sense of the general direction we are heading in but we have no idea about the precise route and destination.

Later on, I quote Markus Reckling, an executive from Deutsche Post who said something very wise to me in one of the interviews for this book. 'I used to think strategy was about avoiding unforeseen circumstances,' he said. 'Now I think it's about making sure you can deal with them.'

And that is the challenge for executives everywhere. Not to spend months or years debating what will or won't happen, but to act now to make your business as fit as possible for whatever might crop up.

What we can be sure of is that the era of creative disruption involves a fundamental change in the way that people engage with each

" the era of creative disruption has only just begun "

other, with corporations and with governments. It involves wave after wave of innovation and entrepreneurship – and traumatic times for many institutions that once seemed invulnerable. It is chaotic, energising and challenging all at the same time. It has echoes of the kind of transformations our forefathers saw as a result of the Industrial Revolution or the arrival of the railways or the car. Most importantly for the purpose of this book, I predict that the era of creative disruption has only really just begun.

The question then is what can any organisation that is caught up in it do about it, and this is what we turn to next.

3

The incumbent's dilemma – and solution

S o, what do you do when you find your core business structurally challenged by the internet, you see swarms of new competitors around you, and your digital business just isn't getting big enough quick enough? As I mentioned in Chapter 1, one of the reasons I started to write this book is that I have found remarkably little in the way of useful advice that chimed with what I was experiencing at the coal face. I found no shortage of what I call 'merchants of hindsight', capable of describing in eloquent detail why disrupted businesses were in trouble and what they should have done 20 years ago. But, this is at best of marginal use. Even the most gifted of CEOs cannot turn back the clock. For better or worse, we have to deal with the businesses we've got and work from there.

There is a view that any attempt to fix the business is a waste of time and effort. Your traditional business should just be managed for cash and then shut down. This, incidentally, was exactly the advice that Michael Dell gave to Apple in 1997.[1] It is true that there are some businesses for whom this is the best option. Their chances of creating a digital future are slim at best. But, like Apple, there are many more who still have plenty to fight for. Their investors deserve nothing less.

---

1 Speaking at the Gartner ITXPO conference in October 1997, Dell was asked what he'd do if he woke up one morning in the body of Steve Jobs, he responded: 'I'd shut [Apple] down and give the money back to shareholders.'

Clayton Christensen, who defined the notion of 'disruptive innovation', takes exactly the opposite approach. He suggests a solution through innovation: more specifically that you should disrupt yourself, often by setting up or acquiring a rival business to your own which will one day become even bigger than the core. As John Taysom, who established Reuters Venture Fund describes it: 'Dream your worst nightmare and then invest in it.'[2] Well, up to a point. In Chapter 4 I talk about Auto Trader (part owned by the Guardian Media Group) which successfully did just that. It built its digital business in competition with its print business, and ultimately increased its overall margins and profits as a result.

But examples like Auto Trader are very thin on the ground. What has happened in this era of internet fuelled disruption is that much activity like this starts out small and stays that way, and as a chief executive, you are still left with the challenge of managing your core business that accounts for the majority of your revenues and profits through the most turbulent period in its history. Self-disruption has an important role to play, and Christensen's approach to innovation is among the best out there. But my close-up experience is that this is all too often only part of the overall plan that a chief executive has to put in place.

Another popular notion is to look at the world of successful internet companies and start-ups and use them as your role model. This is something I have personally fallen for many times over. You look at a dazzling start-up, often one that has come into your sector, and you ask: 'Why can't we be more like that?' There is a very simple and unfortunate answer to this question: 'Because you have absolutely nothing in common with each other.'

&& we ignore the fundamental differences in corporate DNA at our peril 55

A business with a legacy of costs, systems, people and products in need of reinvention is nothing like a business without any of these worries. There are always lessons to learn from successful companies

---

2 In an interview with the author.

of all shapes and sizes, but we ignore the fundamental differences in corporate DNA at our peril. Google has a host of great practices about innovation, and ways of working that have helped to make it the phenomenon it is. But these all sit on top of a massively profitable search advertising business. To think you can adopt the former without the latter, and somehow radically reverse your fortunes as a result, is as misguided as watching a *Superman* movie, putting on a red cape and assuming you will be able to run as fast as a speeding bullet.

Should we look at disrupted internet businesses as role models? The problem is that those who have found themselves in trouble are still in it. Yahoo! is perhaps the most visible example; this is how one analyst described their situation early in 2010:

Yahoo! is weighed down today by dozens of code bases, thousands of revenue-producing properties, at least three sales force factions (display, search, and network), and a few thousand 'extra' employees needed to run the media company today due to its complicated legacy assets and far-flung acquisitions.[3]

These are many of the characteristics of the most challenged of traditional businesses, but Yahoo! hasn't yet provided us with a blueprint for solving them. It just reminds those of us with our roots in the analogue world that digital businesses – even those that were spectacularly successful in their time – can fall prey to creative disruption as well. This is both a consolation, and as our businesses become increasingly digital, a warning of challenges ahead.

So where do we turn? I have spent my time looking at a range of businesses that have found their core business element structurally challenged or in rapid decline. What becomes clear as you look at one example after another is the spectacular challenges that this kind of disruption can cause, and the often traumatic process of recovery and reinvention that has to follow.

---

3 Analyst report on Yahoo! by Jordan Rohan at Thomas Weisel Partners, quoted in TechCrunch at http://techcrunch.com/2010/02/27/ the-steady-efficient-decline-of-Yahoo!

In this section I want to look at four businesses that exemplify this perfectly. The first is Encyclopaedia Britannica. I have long been obsessed at finding out about how Britannica have managed to survive the spectacular disruption they faced, first from the launch of Microsoft's Encarta and then from Wikipedia – and where this has left them as a business. The quick answer is that Britannica have lost 80% of their revenues over 20 years, but they are profitable and growing. This might sound horrific, but the reinvention of their business is, in its own way, a striking success, and one I suspect that many other organisations facing creative disruption will be lucky to emulate.

Next I look at two of the most famous technology turnarounds: IBM and Apple. In both cases, companies that had once been leaders in their field found themselves making a loss and on the brink of collapse, but in both cases they went on to be stronger than they had ever been. It's true that these two lie outside my definition of creative disruption – but the lessons from the coal face of their reinvention are phenomenally relevant.

Finally, I look at the UK's leading music, DVD and book retailer, the HMV Group. Having dominated the high street for decades and seen off challenges from Richard Branson's Virgin Group and the arrival of Tower Records in the UK, with the arrival of the internet it faced a whole new set of challenges.

My conclusions? The most successful recoveries tend to come from businesses that go through three processes of reinvention.

- They transform their core business.
- They find big adjacencies.
- They innovate in the edges.

In Chapters 5–7 we'll look at each of these processes in much more detail. But first, a look at a business that knows more about being disrupted than most of us will ever want or hope to experience: Encyclopaedia Britannica.

Britannica: an educational experience

There is perhaps no single business that exemplifies the traumas a traditional business can experience in the digital age as well as Encyclopaedia Britannica. In the 1980s it was a brilliant business selling $1,000, 30-volume encyclopaedias. Editorially, it was peerless. Contributors had included Sigmund Freud, Albert Einstein and Leon Trotsky; and every article was checked with 17 silent readings by its editors. Commercially, it was a well-oiled sales machine. Leads were generated from print advertising, collated centrally and farmed out to the door-to-door sales team. They would offer a well prepared spiel explaining to aspirational parents that $1,000 was a small price to pay for a child's education, and they earned hundreds of dollars' commission with every sale.

In the early 1990s, however, the business was ravaged by the arrival of the CD-rom and, in particular, by Microsoft's Encarta which sold at a fraction of the price of a print encyclopedia. Encarta went from $395, to $129, to $99 and then down to $50. Millions of copies were sold or given away free with PCs. This was not a money maker for Microsoft but it helped to drive Bill Gates' vision of a PC in every home. Parents, meanwhile, decided in droves, that if they were going to spend $1,000 on their children's education it would be better spent on a PC rather than an encyclopaedia – especially if the PC came with a free copy of Encarta.

> **the initial pricing was designed to protect the encyclopaedia**

Britannica was no digital slouch. In 1989, they launched the first multimedia CD-rom using their secondary encyclopaedia brand Comptons (partly to avoid devaluing *Encyclopaedia Britannica*, but also because it was too big to fit onto a CD-rom). *Business Week* named it one of their products of the year, but the initial pricing was designed to protect the encyclopaedia – and keep the crucial sales team happy: you either got it free with the print edition or had to pay a staggering $895 for it.

Britannica also had a brilliant Advanced Technology Group in La Jolla, South California, which led the fiendishly difficult process of taking the Britannica database online (one of the main challenges was getting all the special characters and mathematical formulae converted). But La Jolla was a long way from Chicago – geographically and culturally – and according to the company's former editor in chief, Robert McHenry, the business suffered as a result of 'the inability of the company's senior management to embrace electronic publishing and pursue it forcefully'.[4]

Britannica eventually launched its own CD-rom on two discs, and a subscription-based web version of the encyclopaedia, but its business had already been shaken to the core. In 1995 the owner, the William Benton Foundation, sold it to the billionaire Jacob Safra, who started a programme of radical and expensive reinvention. The door-to-door sales team, and the central team that supported Britannica was dismantled, with nearly 2,000 lay-offs. The business was dragged from the print to the digital age.

Britannica launched an edited search engine in partnership with Yahoo! Ultimately it would never have competed with Google, but it never got a chance – when the nascent online advertising market became one of the first victims of the dotcom crash, the project was killed off.

Then came Wikipedia. The impact on Britannica's business was nothing like as dramatic as the chaos wreaked by Encarta, but it profoundly damaged their reputation. Wikipedia was the bottom-up, wisdom-of-the-crowds embodiment of everything that was wonderful about the web. At every opportunity this was compared with Britannica's hierarchical editorial processes. To compound this, in December 2005, highly respected *Nature* magazine ran a 'special report' titled 'Internet encyclopaedias go head to head', with the conclusion that the level of errors in a set of randomly chosen Britannica articles was not a

---

4 http://www.howtoknow.com/BOL1.html

million miles off the number found in a Wikipedia article. Britannica did – and still does – contest the findings (they focused only on scientific articles where Wikipedia's coverage is strong due to the nature of internet users), but the damage was done.

I bought Encarta, and to this day I believe Wikipedia is one of the great phenomena of our age. But I have also always been fascinated by Britannica and how it had surived this onslaught. There has been much written about how the shift from atoms to bytes destroyed the economics of Britannica's business and so, in the summer of 2009, I met with Jorge Cauz, Britannica's president. He had been with the company since 1996, and lived through the pain of restructuring, the challenge of competing with Encarta, and rebuilding the business while the world was turning to Wikipedia.

Speaking to Cauz, I became more convinced than ever about the relevance of Britannica's experience to others. Not just as a cautionary tale of what happens when you get things wrong but, more importantly, as a cautionary tale of what happens *even when you do things right.*

Lesson 1: What success looks like – Britannica's new reality

For me, the fact that Britannica still has a business is a success – especially if you consider the business that the new owners inherited in 1996. But the shape and size of the business in 2010 is very different to what it was even a decade ago. It has been reinvented from top to bottom: people, systems, products and customers have all changed. Here are the bald facts.

■ Britannica's revenues have dropped by approximately 80% since their peak in the early 1990s.

■ They now employ some 240 people rather than more than 2,000. Their editorial team, however, has nearly doubled in size over the period to around 120.

■ After a decade of losses, they have been in profit since 2005, and their revenues are growing again, thanks primarily to online subscriptions in the education and library markets. More than 85% of their revenues are now digital.

- All their editorial processes and systems have had to be changed to enable continuous updating, and editing and writing from users of their website.

To put a positive spin on it, you see a business that is profitable and growing. It has managed to find a relatively stable customer base in the education and professional markets, and has supportive owners. They have survived the most traumatic change they are likely to ever have to experience. The brand is still strong. The world is still hungry for knowledge from trusted sources. I suspect they know more about their customers, consumers and competitors now than they ever did. Not only that, but they outlasted Encarta, which was closed in 2009. But, the business is smaller, much smaller. And I suspect that is going to be the fate of many businesses experiencing the sort of disruption faced by Britannica.

Lesson 2: Just being 'more digital' wouldn't have saved things

Britannica's management made mistakes. Their initial pricing of the Compton's CD-rom was over protective, and designed to keep the sales force happy rather than compete effectively in the new market-place. There was also a fair bit of denial about the impact of the digital world. I can imagine executives (most of whom had come through the salesforce) insisting and believing that clicking your way through a CD-rom would never replace the physical joy of owning and browsing a gorgeous leather backed encyclopaedia. They were hardly alone among executives of the time in overestimating our devotion to physical forms of content.

the result was a dramatic drop in the total market size

But the horrible truth is that with the move to CD-roms and ultimately the internet almost all of Britannica's sources of competitive advantage were shattered. Barriers to entry dropped, and in came a particularly challenging new entrant. Microsoft had the advantages of formidable scale and resource, and no legacy business to worry about. They drove prices down, and ultimately gave Encarta away with new PCs. The result was a dramatic drop in the total market size.

It is hard to grow if your addressable market is shrinking, and the decline in Britannica's headline revenues was much more an indicator of what was happening to their market than a measure of their response to it. And this is is why I am cautious about the belief that just investing in the thing that is going to kill you is enough to secure long-term growth.

Lesson 3: Only a big adjacency move would have made a real difference

When I asked Cauz what they should have done differently, he went back to the late 1980s and early 1990s when the business was good, and there were tons of things one could have done to leverage the brand in the education market. He compared Britannica's fate with the success that the Washington Post company has had with its investment at the time in Kaplan, the education business which now provides the vast majority of their group's profit and has shielded the newspaper through the past decade (see Chapter 6).

Why didn't Britannica make a similar move? They had a formidable brand and plenty of cash. They tried some brand extensions, including a loss-making move into homework centres, and they expanded their publishing portfolio, but none of this had the feeling of being sustained or substantial. So they became a shrinking encyclopaedia business rather than an expanding education business.

Part of the problem is that, at the time, Britannica was a cash cow for a foundation. The trustees wanted to take the cash from the business in order to fulfil their good work. Furthermore, once Safra took hold of the business, then all of the investment rightly had to focus on a costly restructuring and transformation programme, rather than looking for exciting businesses to buy and invest in.

Had Britannica managed to build a growth business alongside the core encyclopaedia business, they might have been able to use this to fuel long-term growth, while continuing with the reinvention of their encyclopaedia business. As we see later when we look at how people chase big adjacencies, this is always a risky strategy: but, as it turned out, not going down this route carried more than its fair share of risk as well.

Lesson 4: The reality of reinvention– legacy systems, clashing priorities, too much to do

In 2008, Britannica announced it would open itself up to Wikipedia-style contributions and editing from its users. It felt like the company had finally acknowledged that there was something worth looking at in the Wikipedia model. The truth was that they had acknowledged this much earlier, but making it happen had been a formidably challenging process.

Cauz had been watching Wikipedia from its earliest days and had always been aware of the potential of the web as a collaborative medium since its development. Britannica, he felt, was a much more collaborative organisation than many gave it credit for, and now it was time to take this type of collaboration into the digital age. So, early in 2005, he planned to lay out his vision of how Britannica should evolve to some of his leading editors and technical staff.

Cauz talked about three big changes to the way their online product worked: first, the need to 'push to publish' – the ability to instantly update their content; second, the need to present profiles of their contributors; finally, the need to show the history of their articles so that readers could see changes that had been made. These were big changes – conceptually and technically. And, as he outlined his plan, he could tell it wasn't going down well in the room:

They looked at me, and I knew I wasn't getting any place. They sort of understood, but they thought it was not really required. We had a ton of other problems to fix. I think ... they interpreted it – rightly so – as a huge amount of work on top of all the other initiatives. We needed to have three products for the institutional market, we were deploying our K-12 product and deploying our library product and at the same time making our college product more robust ... and here comes the CEO and he's talking about publishing immediately, and we need an article history and we need profiles of the contributors, and that's going to take us forever.[5]

After the meeting, Cauz retrenched a bit. He did a bit more explaining to people, talking them through the need to change, and months later in June 2005, the business kicked off – what eventually became known as Project Darwin.

The staff were right, it would take a lot of work. All of Britannica's content sits in a single database and to implement these sort of changes while they were still developing other projects was like performing open heart surgery on a patient while she is running a marathon. It took the best part of three years before the results were announced.

This is the difference between reinvention and starting from a blank sheet of paper. It is also the difference between being inside a company and outside it. On the outside the idea seems like simplicity itself. On the inside, even an obvious change feels like moving mountains. Should Britannica have delivered this change sooner? Definitely. Could they have? Unlikely.

For incumbents, ideas about transformation are easy. The challenge is all about making them happen: a process that often raises massive technological and human challenges.

Lesson 5: Your reputation is everything, protect it with your life

When I speak to people about Britannica, their first shock is that they still have a business; the next shock is when I tell them it is profitable. The final shock is when I tell them that I met Jorge Cauz and found him to be a really smart and engaging business leader – as switched

---

5 Jorge Cauz in conversation with the author.

on to the internet as any executive I have come across. Everyone who is vaguely interested in this world, should know those three facts. But partly, I suspect, because of their private ownership, partly because they're constantly under the cosh, Britannica have tended to keep their light under a bushel.

❝ Encarta took a knife to Britannica's revenues ❞

Encarta took a knife to Britannica's revenues; Wikipedia did that to Britannica's reputation. To put it mildly, it has proved something of a PR challenge for Britannica. They have been endlessly drawn into squabbles about different editing methods and levels of accuracy. And, to act as a merchant of hindsight myself, it's clear that there have been mistakes along the way. When *Nature* magazine ran its comparison of Wikipedia and Britannica it gave the damning verdict that:

'*Wikipedia* comes close to *Britannica* in terms of the accuracy of its science entries.'[6]

The impact was instant, but it took Britannica nearly three months to respond in full. They delivered a 20-page academic rebuttal, but by then the damage had been done, as they admitted:

Within hours of the article's appearance on *Nature*'s website, media organisations worldwide proclaimed that *Wikipedia* was almost as accurate as the oldest continuously published reference work in the English language.[7]

They had been attacked in internet time; they responded in encyclopaedia time.

How you are perceived as a business matters at the best of times: it affects how your customers see you and how your employees feel about what they're doing. It takes on a new urgency and importance

---

6 'Internet Encyclopaedias Go Head to Head', *Nature*, 438, 15 December 2005.
7 'Fatally Flawed: Refuting the recent study on encyclopaedia accuracy by the journal Nature', *Encyclopaedia Britannica*, March 2006.

when your business is facing disruption. No-one wants to feel they're on the losing side; and too often Britannica has been put in the position of the reactionary force, clinging on to outmoded ways of doing things.

The key task is to project your business as part of the future, not simply to be a critic of the present or defender of the past, and to do so using all the tools available. In a world of blogs and social media, a few of the right things, said in the right way and in the right place, can have a dramatic impact on how you're perceived.

I liked Cauz. I'm glad Britannica is still in business and I hope it prospers. Wikipedia is a thing of wonder, it has taken reference way beyond the realm of the traditional encyclopaedia, but the idea that it becomes the only reference work on the planet is as worrying as any monopoly. Jacob Safra has also clearly been a good proprietor and funded Britannica's transformation – and that has been a critical factor in their progress to date.

But, more than anything, Britannica's tale shows the brutal reality of surviving disruption. The most telling comment actually came from their PR man, the charming Tom Panelas who has been with the company throughout: 'There's no end of armchair experts telling us what we should do or should have done, but the truth is that we just have to grind it out.'[8] Too true.

IBM and Apple: lessons from big tech turnarounds

The corporate graveyard around Silicon Valley is full of businesses that didn't make it from one wave of technology to the next. Some disappear altogether; others shrink, struggle and end up acquired and absorbed by those who are either on the up, or simply more resistant.

In the mid 1990s, it looked like there were two more businesses that would suffer this fate: IBM and Apple. Both were on the brink of

8 In conversation with the author.

collapse. A decade later, they had become two of the most successful technology businesses in the world and, as I have been writing this book, they have both continued to deliver one set of record earnings after another.

The management challenges IBM and Apple faced are very relevant to businesses trapped in the current world of creative disruption. The businesses that had stood them in good stead for years were crumbling around them – and we find chief executives who had to transform big, complex organisations, often with many of their executive teams and staff throughout the businesses wedded to the glories of the past. They had to build new businesses while managing old ones, and do it on a massive scale. And, in all cases, they had to do it within the visibility of the capital markets.

So, how did they do it, and what can we learn from each company?

IBM – surviving the ultimate disruption

If you want to find the perfect example of disruptive innovation, it is the impact that the PC had on the mainframe world. IBM, as we know it, was built on the back of a mainframe computer, the System/360. It was the result of billions of dollars of R&D and announced to the world on April 1964. In the press release for its launch IBM's chairman Thomas J. Watson Jr announced: 'This is the beginning of a new generation – not only of computers – but of their application in business, science and government.' This was not an exaggeration. For nearly 30 years, IBM mainframes led the world, and they became one of the planet's most successful businesses as a result – driving the spread of mainframe computers throughout the corporate world in the 1970s and 1980s.

By the early 1990s, however, things were not going so well. Mainframe sales were in freefall, thanks to a triple whammy. First came the arrival of Unix, an open standard which broke IBM's end-to-end proprietary stranglehold on the market. Next came serious price competition in the mainframe market from the likes of Hitachi, Fujitsu and Amdahl.

The final body blow came from the rise of the PC and its elevation from a hobbyist's machine to a serious business tool.

In 1991, for the first time ever, IBM's sales went backward, falling by 6.1%, and the company made its first annual loss. Sales in its core hardware division were down by 15.9%, a catastrophic and unprecedented drop. Things did not improve. In January 1993, IBM hit the headlines for all the wrong reasons: it announced a $5bn loss for the previous year, which at the time was the largest loss in US corporate history.

Into this fray stepped Louis V. Gerstner Jr as CEO. He had previously been CEO of RJR Nabisco after stints as a senior executive at American Express and time as a McKinsey consultant. He was not a technologist and initially was reluctant to take on the job, but he was seduced by the need for a new challenge, the compelling arguments of key members of the board, and partly out a sense of patriotism. ('If IBM fails, it won't be good for America,' he was told by one director.)

❝ over a decade, Gerstner transformed IBM ❞

Over a decade, Gerstner transformed IBM from a bureaucratic monolith on the way to oblivion into a modern IT giant. In 2008, some 15 years after everyone thought IBM should have been broken up, the company reported record pre-tax income of £16.7bn – a seventh consecutive year of double-digit income growth. The very simple narrative is that Gerstner found a dying mainframe business, and in its place he built a services business which is now the backbone of modern IBM. But no-one gets to walk into a business the size of IBM and just wave a magic wand. As you look into that period of the company's history in more detail, you realise that what really happened is slightly more nuanced – and, I believe, even more relevant for many businesses in other sectors.

Detailed analysis and action, not vision

As he was announcing his change programme to the press, Gerstner famously said: 'The last thing IBM needs right now is a vision.' The comment was picked up and criticised – often by journalists who tend to like leaders who are high on vision. Gerstner's point was that there was no shortage of vision statements from IBM in the past, but this was a business in crisis and what it needed was a thoroughly thought through plan and a real focus on execution of that plan:

Truly great companies lay out strategies that are believable and executable.... Good strategies are long on detail and short on vision.[9]

In truth, the plan Gerstner put in place for IBM, of a new, energised business focused on software and services growing from within the business, was genuinely bold and visionary. The focus, however, was on analysis and action, and preparing the business for what he believed to be the future (in particular the world of networked computing and global businesses) rather than soul searching meaningless mission statements or simply trying to rekindle past glories.

The big bet – keep the business together and invest in the mainframe

When he arrived, everyone was telling Gerstner to break IBM up. The media and analysts thought it was inevitable and many IBM executives were busy rebranding their divisions ready for such a break up. Gerstner's big decision was to hold the business together, believing that in an increasingly open and fragmented computing world there would be a need for an integrator to bring everything together – and that would be IBM's role.

The other generally perceived wisdom was that the mainframe was dying. But when Gerstner got into the business he realised he couldn't walk away from the market. And, when he spoke to customers (the CIOs and CTOs of major corporations) he found them annoyed that IBM wasn't doing more to stand up for the mainframe. Rather than walking away Gerstner backed a proposal that had already gone to the board, to invest $1bn over the next four years in their mainframe business on a risky project to convert from one type of technical archi-

---

9 This quote and others in this section come from Lou Gerstner's gripping account of his time at IBM, *Who Says Elephants Can't Dance?* (2003, HarperCollins).

tecture (bipolar) to another (CMOS – complementary metal oxide semiconductor).

With CMOS, IBM was able to drop the prices on their mainframes, and keep a decent gross margin. The project delivered. Over seven years, the cost of a unit of processing power dropped from $63,000 to $2,500 allowing IBM to remain competitive, and even now it still sells mainframes. By giving the core business an extra lease of life, Gerstner bought the time – and the cashflow – that allowed the business to change. 'This program, probably more than any other, saved IBM,' Gerstner said in his memoirs.

In both of these examples Gerstner went against the groupthink of analysts and commentators: in both cases he was right.

Change the organisation – from the top down

Gerstner found a business that was riddled with bureaucracy and burdened with a cost base it could no longer afford. He immediately and decisively set about changing the organisation at every level with a massive programme of corporate re-engineering.

As he recalls in his memoirs: 'At any given time more than 60 major re-engineering projects were underway – and hundreds more among individual units and divisions.'

Among Gerstner's first moves were a set of decisions designed to break down some of these fiefdoms and create a more dynamic environment. He started from the top by reducing the total number of board members (previously 18), and changed some of the board personnel. He also abandoned the powerful six-man Management Committee, the most senior executive decision-making body in the organisation. This had been intended as a forum for collective decision making and internal challenge – part of a system of contention where line managers could openly challenge each other in a system of peer review. But, over time, it had become heavily politicised, and in the end it drove compromises rather than bold decision making. Executives developed what Gerstner described as a 'system of prearranged consensus' that ultimately 'diffused responsibility and leadership'. It had to go – and its end was a potent symbol of change within the organisation.

IBM was structured by geographic region, but Gerstner soon realised this resulted in a set of fiefdoms that stopped the business acting in an integrated way (at one point he found out that the head of his European operation had been blocking his all-staff emails as he thought 'they weren't right for my staff'). To break this up and meet his customers' increasingly global needs, he restructured the business by industry sector (Finance, Government, Media) instead.

As well as getting the structure right Gerstner had to get the cost base in order. He talked about right-sizing the business in his first meeting with the executive team – and although in the long term the company grew under him, in the short term he had to take cost out to improve the cashflow situation.

For the first time under new CFO Jerry York the business bench-marked its cost base against its competitors and found that IBM's cost to generate a dollar of revenue was around 42 cents, compared to an average of 31 cents among their competitors. Multiplied up that meant an annual overspend of $7bn. The result was an $8.9bn cost reduction plan. Some 45,000 jobs had gone in 1992, and another 35,000 had to go as well. Some $2bn was saved from IT expenses. The 240 people running the real estate and construction operation was reduced through outsourcing to just 42, and 8,000 acres of undeveloped land were sold off.

Build and buy the new business – services and software

IBM's services business was small but growing rapidly when Gerstner arrived. By the time he left, nearly half of IBM's workforce was working in services. In 2008, the service business accounted for 42% of pre-tax income – its largest segment. The services business was taken to a new level in 2002 (after Gerstner had moved on) with the acquisition of PWC Consulting for $3.5bn.

The problem with building a services business within IBM is that the services team would regularly recommend suppliers other than IBM; which, of course, infuriated the sales team who were out there trying to shift as much IBM product as possible. The standard theory here is that you should set the services business up as a separate unit, but Gerstner kept it within the sales team until it had reached scale and then let it become its own division, even though this meant that nearly every week there was a major conflagration between the sales and services elements that he had to quell.

The other new area came from developing the software business. The major move here was the $3.2bn acquisition of Lotus Development Corporation in 1995. And over the years there would be dozens of different acquisitions to build up the software portfolio. But in one way IBM also got out of the software business – by stopping developing their own HR, Finance and ERP applications.

This software was all proprietary for IBM machines, but it wasn't going well. Their applications weren't the leaders, and when Gerstner's executives carried out an audit they found that IBM had invested some $20bn in software, with a return rate of -70%. Even worse, by following this strategy IBM were creating enemies in some of the world's biggest software businesses. And the problem was that as people tended to chose their application first, and their hardware to fit with it, everyone was making their software incompatible with IBM's hardware.

The answer? Yes there were some smaller acquisitions, but when it came to working with major players such as SAP and Oracle, in the end IBM went down a less costly and more effective route – they set up a series of formal partnerships with key applications providers. Thus IBM benefited both from the resulting hardware sales, and from the service and support agreements for the whole technical stack.

Excitement at the edges

It was during Gerstner's time in office that the internet came to prominence. It is easy to forget that for many of those involved with 'serious' computing, the internet, with its open standards, barely registered.

As an early internet adopter, however, I remember changing my view of IBM as a result of two events – the website for when their Big Blue supercomputer beat Kasparov, and the fact that they ran brilliant websites for the 1996 Olympics and Wimbledon. This activity was the exact opposite of the top-down, 'big bet' work that was put in gear by Gerstner. It came from a small entrepreneurial team that begged and borrowed resource, and hacked code together in the nick of time (the Big Blue site was launched after the original one, from an external agency, but collapsed within days).

Gary Hamel's excellent paper 'Waking Up IBM'[10] describes how this happened within IBM – thanks mainly to a senior strategy executive John Patrick, and one of their programmers, David Grossman. Together Grossman and Patrick created a 'Get Connected' manifesto for IBM, and built up a virtual 'Get Connected' team of a few hundred IBMers who tirelessly campaigned to make IBM a meaningful player in the online world. After working under the radar for months, they took their plan for an IBM site to Gerstner who instantly gave his approval.

Even after that, however, Grossman and Patrick still had to secure approval and they presented to IBM's top 300 officers in May 1994, showing them the proposed IBM website and those by Hewlett Packard, Sun Microsystems and, just to rub it in, one created by Grossman's six-year-old son. Patrick recalls the reaction:

A lot of people were saying 'how do you make money at this?' I said,
'I have no idea. All I know is that this is the most powerful, important

---

10 Gary Hamel (2000) 'Waking Up IBM', *Harvard Business Review*, June,
http://hbr.org/2000/07/waking-up-ibm/ar/1

form of communication both inside and outside the company that has ever existed.'[11]

Gerstner's role here was one of continuous support. He had flagged the importance of networked computing on his arrival, and the internet fitted with this. He insisted that all financial reports went up on the IBM website, and during the hostile takeover of Lotus in 1995, all the proposals from IBM went online instantly. Today, of course, this is standard behaviour – but back then it was radical stuff – particularly coming from a CEO.

The benefit of this work wasn't just the development of a powerful communication channel. Many of the products developed by Grossman and his team for their Olympic websites became mainstream IBM products, and within a few years, 'e-business' was a key element of IBM's brand positioning – convincing the world that they were the people to do business with if you needed to have a serious online presence. By the end of 1998, IBM had completed 18,000 e-business consulting engagements.

❝ 'e-business' was a key element of IBM's brand positioning ❞

Rebuild the brand

When Gerstner took over, the US business alone had 70 ad agencies. He found that some months industry magazines would carry page after page of IBM advertising from different business units, often with different messaging and logos. Other months there would be nothing.

Gerstner allocated all of IBM's advertising globally to one agency, Ogilvy & Mather. A massive call – especially as the decision was made on personal chemistry rather than the presentation of screeds of creative work. The first result to the external world was a campaign under the banner 'solutions for a small planet' that kick started the process of getting people to think again about IBM, which had recently been a by-word for corporate failure. Even though the company was

---

11 Ibid.

going through organisational turmoil as it evolved, a mix of the right agency and the right message could start the vital job of changing the world's perception of IBM.

The relationship with Ogilvy & Mather is still in place over 15 years later.

Bringing Apple back from the brink

People often look at Apple's recovery and focus on the wave of brilliant products that were launched since Steve Jobs reappeared in the business: the iMac, iPod, iPhone and iPad. No company on the planet has quite been able to match Apple's skills in creating genre-defining consumer electronics products.

Much of what they have achieved is down to Steve Jobs himself, and the creative genius of their design guru Jonathan Ive. But the period I'm fascinated with is the period between Apple's near collapse in 1995 and the launch of the first iMac in 1998. This was the period that saved Apple and laid the foundation for the brilliance we see today. And it also provides a blueprint for what you have to do to a company that has completely lost its way.

The brink of disaster

In 1995, Michael Spindler, the CEO of Apple Computing, and Joe Graziano, the company's CFO had decided that the only way forward for their once great business was to sell it. Apple was in a terrible state. Despite record sales figures the company had declared a $69m loss in the final quarter and their share of the personal computer market had dropped from around 20% in the early 1980s to below 8%, and there were 1,600 lay-offs under way. In addition, there were problems with the supply chain: Apple had suffered from three quarters of product shortages, and then a quarter of surplus inventory.

True Apple had the best brand and the most loyal consumers, and a strong position in the education market, 'assets that other businesses would kill for' Compaq chairman Benjamin M. Rosen told *Business*

Week[12] at the time – and these would ultimately provide the basis for a recovery, but they weren't enough to get them out of their immediate crisis.

On 23 January 1996 Apple held a board meeting in New York. Scott McNealy, the co-founder of Sun attended. With the stock trading at $28 a share, he offered $23. The offer was rejected. The board then decided that Spindler's time as CEO was over, and that Gil Amelio, at the time CEO of National Semiconductors, should take over.

Give it to Gil

Apple was not facing the same sort of structural challenge as IBM. In fact they were already sitting in the fastest growing market of all – personal computing – but the business had lost both direction and momentum, and when Amelio took the helm, it was also starting to lose serious money.

Amelio had done a brilliant job at National Semiconductors: the stock price had gone up four-fold since his arrival. There was no doubting his capability to turn a technology business round – but whether or not he could turn Apple round was another matter.

Amelio's book *In the Firing Line: My 500 days at Apple* is a classic study in CEO frustration. He finds a company that was profoundly dysfunctional. Every internal meeting ends up being leaked. Cost control of the wrong kind means products are shipping that are at best sub-par, and certainly not up to Apple's standards. This was his recollection of the business he joined:

Apple was manufacturing the wrong products with the wrong features, in the wrong quantities, marred with severe quality problems. The warehouses were stuffed with $600m worth of unsalable computers. The hard cash reserves were so low that the company could not survive more than another four months. Executives made decisions based on what was right for their own operation, not what was right for the company.

---

12 www.businessweek.com/archives/1996/b3460044.arc.htm

And the culture stressed the individual and freedom of action instead of cooperation and working toward a set of common goals.[13]

> After his four months of strategy work, carried out in a secret bunker that only further distanced him and his inner team from the business, he revealed his white paper on the future of the business to the board who did not seem particularly thrilled. When he arranged to present it to his senior management team many of them simply did not show up.

> At the 1997 MacWorld, Amelio told the gathered army of Mac fans: 'It's chaos, but I love it.' Reading his book, you suspect there was a fair bit of exaggeration in the second part of that statement. But, for all his misery, he did start to get the business into shape. For a start, he took a considerable amount of cost out of the business – cutting staff numbers by about 5,000 – or about 25% of the business – and crucially he sorted out the parlous state of the balance sheet by securing $650m in funding (something that he says secured his one and only compliment from Steve Jobs).

❝ Copeland was going nowhere ❞

Amelio also brought in a new CTO, Ellen Hancock, and with her spotted that the project for the new Mac operating system, Copeland, was going nowhere. It was massively late and over budget. Instead he found the solution by acquiring NeXT, the nascent operating system being developed by Apple founder Steve Jobs.

The awkward inter-regnum

As part of the NeXT deal Amelio then invited Jobs in to act as his adviser on a temporary basis. Immediately, the press attention focused on the relationship between the two men, and in particular what Jobs was planning to do. Jobs was keen to quash rumours that he was planning to single handedly save the company, and return as CEO: 'They want me to be some kind of Superman.' He said, 'But I have

---

13 Gil Amelio (1999) *On the Firing Line: My 500 Days at Apple*, Harper Paperbacks, p. 271.

no desire to run Apple Computer. I deny it at every turn, but nobody believes me.'[14]

Amelio, meanwhile realised that if he was going to succeed in a business such as Apple, he needed some of Jobs' magic: 'If the price for getting Apple healthy is involving Steve ... I'm O.K. with that. I'm a big boy,' he said at the time.[15]

First came tussles over personnel. Jobs saw that Ellen Hancock (who he had described to a journalist as a 'bozo') and Marco Landi, Amelio's COO, were both effectively demoted – Hancock was taken off R&D and Landi was made head of sales, and then resigned. Jobs had some of his key lieutentants from NeXT put in charge of developing Apple's new hardware and operating systems. But beyond the personality tussle, Jobs started to sort out the mess around Apple's product line.

One of his first moves was one of the most surprising. The man whose company would become a by-word for innovation cut the R&D budget by 50%. His principle was that people should be working on great Mac products for right now, rather than advanced research that might never see the light of day.

But the partnership between Jobs and Amelio was never going to work, and there was only going to be one winner. Amelio was fired in July 1997. Jobs stood in, initially as 'acting CEO'.

Jobs takes the reins and prepares for greatness

Now in charge, Jobs' first task was trimming down the business even further. In all, the number of hardware lines at Apple went down from 17 in 1997 to five by early 1998. A whole heap of Macs in their product range were put into retirement. The Apple Newton, a bulky handheld device, disappeared as did the eMate laptop for schools, and a raft of other nondescript mid-range boxes.

---

14 http://www.businessweek.com/1997/11/b3518120.htm
15 Ibid.

Software projects such as the Cyberdog internet suite were killed off and about 700 staff lost their jobs when he brought the software subsidiary Claris back into the business. Jobs also scrapped the 'cloning' strategy that allowed other manufacturers to make machines with the Apple operating system inside. This had been introduced in 1994 – under Michael Spindler – and designed as a way to give Apple's operating system the sort of ubiquity that Microsoft Windows enjoyed, but Jobs believed it was simply taking hardware sales away from Apple.

After years of only ever seeing Microsoft as the enemy, Jobs announced a partnership with them, inviting Bill Gates onto the stage at the MacWorld in 1997 (a partnership that Amelio says he laid the ground for).

Jobs brought in Tim Cook, who has since become the company's powerful COO, to sort out the supply chain – dramatically improving the product consistency, quality and profitability. He outsourced manufacturing and also took a leaf out of Dell's book by allowing people to configure their machines online with the launch of the Apple Store. And, before he really had much in the way of great product to boast about, he moved his advertising business to the agency TBWA and launched one of the best ad campaigns in history: 'Think Different' featuring the likes of Einstein and Ghandi gave the brand the sort of alternative allure that had eluded it for years.

When Apple started to deliver a profit, it did so against a background of falling sales. They were leaner and smarter and focused on profitable products, such as the new PowerMac G3. But, this wasn't simply about great product, this was about good business.

In 1998, Steve Jobs revealed the iMac in its candy coloured gloriousness – and in doing so changed Apple's fortunes. The iPod would follow soon after and the iPhone after that. Apple as we now know it had been born.

Six lessons from Apple and IBM

1 You can't recreate the past, you have to build a future

IBM and Apple had a huge amount in their histories to be proud of. But, by the time that Gerstner and Amelio walked in their respective doors, those past glories were gone, and they weren't coming back. As leaders, they both embodied breaks from the past; and the symbolism of their appointments was a critical message – both to those inside and outside the organisation.

strong brands, loyal customers and great brains provide a platform for the future In both cases though, the challenge was to use the past as an asset, but not let it become a millstone. Strong brands, loyal customers and great brains inside the business provide a platform for the future – but they do not on their own provide a solution. At the same time, there can be no tolerance of organisational structures and behaviours that come from a different time but now stop the decision making and collaboration required for radical transformation.

2 Getting the core business into shape is essential, but not enough

It was essential for Gerstner to take out cost and reinvest in the mainframe, but ultimately it was the services and software business that saved him. He had to do both in order to succeed. Similarly, it was critical for Amelio to make Apple a smaller business and sort out the balance sheet, and for Jobs to trim back the core product line and sort out the supply chain, but ultimately it took the iMac, and then the more radical leaps of the iPod and iPhone, to make Apple the powerhouse we now know.

Jobs had seen this from outside the company. Interviewed in *Fortune* in 1996 he said: 'If I were running Apple, I would milk the Macintosh for all it's worth and get busy on the next great thing. The PC wars are over. Done. Microsoft won a long time ago.'[16] He knew that the

---

16 Quoted in 'Paradise Lost', *Fortune*, 19 February 1996.

future lay beyond the PC, but the first thing he did was sort out Apple's computer business. First, economically with the launch of the profitable G3, then creatively with the launch of the iMac.

Both businesses had to step beyond their traditional comfort zones in order to get back to growth, but they could only do that once they had sorted out their core businesses. Trying to reach out into new areas before sorting out the core is like building a skyscraper on quicksand. Exciting, perhaps, but destined to fail.

3   The need for the right leader in the right place at the right time

These are both tales of leadership – and whether it was Gerstner, Amelio or Jobs – all three were committed to overturning the status quo that had got their businesses into trouble and to building something new. Gerstner was able to do so as the ultimate outsider, bringing to bear his experience as a customer rather than as a technologist. Jobs was able to do this as an insider – demanding perfection and leading a revolution in Apple's product line-up.

Amelio played a key role in Apple's reinvention and has been keen to make that point. In an interview three years after he left he said of Jobs: 'I should get all the credit for making [his work] possible.'[17] 'All' is possibly over-egging it, but he has a point.

That said, in his hands, Apple would probably never have delivered the iMac, iPod, iPhone or Apple's truly brilliant advertising work. With time, Amelio might have been able to turn Apple back into a good company. But it took Steve Jobs to turn it into a truly great company.

4   The importance of a strong brand in tough times

In both cases, the Apple and IBM brands carried massive value – but like the businesses around them they had fallen on hard times. The

---

17 Douglas Harbrecht (ed.) (2000) 'What Gil Amelio thinks of Steve Jobs now', Newsmaker Q&A, *Business Week*, 21 January www.businessweek.com/print/ bwdaily/dnflash/jan2000/nf00121e.htm?chan=db

investment in the brand was a critical part of their turnarounds. Both companies switched ad agencies and came out with very big, bold consistent messaging right in the middle of their turnarounds. Apple's 'Think Different' and IBM's 'Solutions for a small planet' managed in both cases to capture the change that was happening within the organisations and project it to the outside world ahead of any major shift in product line-up or change in financial fortunes.

And in these fickle times, both Apple and IBM are still with the ad agencies that came up with those campaigns.

5 'Innovation' is there to serve the business, not the other way round

When Gerstner joined IBM, the business was on its knees, but they were just celebrating a year of having more patents registered in the US than any other company. Their academic R&D efforts were peerless, but it was doing them no good.

Similarly, at Apple, $30m a year was being spent on advanced research, but they couldn't get their next operating system out on time. So Jobs dramatically reduced the amount of investment in advanced research – he wanted all efforts to go into the next Mac product, not into blue sky thinking. The point is that when times are good and there is spare cash around, all of this innovation and R&D can add a healthy glow to the business, but when things are against you it's a luxury you can't afford.

There still has to be a focus on innovation – but this has to be a focus on delivering distinctive, innovative products to market. As we will see later, 'innovation' is either there to help you transform your core business, or to help you break into adjacent markets. And, if it isn't doing either of these things, it is redundant.

6 The biggest test of a turnaround is what happens next

The kind of reinvention that happened at Apple and IBM was not simply about a process of change happening between two points in time. It is about creating an organisation that behaves in a different way, and, hopefully, won't allow itself to get into the same mess in which it once found itself.

Probably Gerstner's greatest achievement was not what happened when he was there, but what happened after he left. He handed over to an internal successor, Sam Palmisano, in 2002, and the business has travelled along the same fundamental lines, continuing to evolve and prosper. Similarly, the greatest test of Steve Jobs' time at Apple will be whether Apple will continue to deliver products that define its markets after he has decided to step down.

“ in the world of technology, continuous innovation is the norm ”

In the world of technology, it is given that everything has a finite lifespan and continuous innovation is the norm. But for many incumbent businesses in other sectors, the new physics of business we now operate in come as a sharp shock. With the leap from physical to digital comes a new intensity in their competitive environment, and, as a result, a step change in the need to innovate, react to opportunities and threats, and respond to their customers' wants and needs.

HMV: reinventing a fallen retail hero

Our next case picks up on many of the themes we have already seen in action: in particular the need to focus on transforming the core business. This considers the HMV Group, which owns the entertainment retailer HMV and the UK's largest book retailer, Waterstones. It is the UK business that is most affected by the resurgence of Apple and the rise of Amazon.

From hero to zero and back again

HMV was one of the great successes of the British high street and for anyone who loved music, visits to its vast stores were one of the Saturday afternoon rituals of growing up.

The business was launched in 1821, but it was in the 1960s that HMV started to expand throughout the UK, going through a massive growth surge in the 1980s and 1990s by moving into new cities and bigger stores. They set up operations in Canada, Japan and the USA, and they survived the challenges of Richard Branson's Virgin Megastores and the arrival of Tower Records from the USA.

The business had been part of EMI (or Thorn EMI as it was), but in 1998, after a leveraged buy-out, it became the HMV Group. They had already moved into book retailing before buying the country's largest specialist book retailer, Waterstones, from WH Smiths. In 2002 HMV went public and on the day of the flotation the company was worth around £700m.

In 2010 that valuation had become about £260m. A decade of dealing with music piracy, and the growth of Amazon, Apple's iTunes and supermarkets selling cut price books, CDs, DVDs and computer games has left HMV operating in a very different world to the one where they experienced their golden years. As consumers have been given ever greater choice about how, where and when they get their entertainment, HMV has been structurally weakened.

The challenges faced by the business really started to come through in the group's 2005/06 results. Like-for-like sales and profits were down. Operating profit at the core UK HMV business was down by 35% and they had to downgrade their forecasts for the growth of HMV Digital which had only launched a few months earlier.

Alan Giles, the CEO who had brought the group together and seen it through flotation, had signalled he was planning to step down – and, in July 2006, he named his successor, Simon Fox, who had been COO of the white goods retailer Kesa.

Fox joined in October 2006 and within six months, he found himself having to go to the market with his second profit warning. Things were not going well. It was becoming clear that the business was really feeling the impact of both the internet and the growth of supermarkets – and as a result, the magic that had worked in the past, wasn't going to work in the future. Investors needed to know what Fox was going to do about it, and so did his staff. Fox recalls:

There was a lot of pressure to have a three-year plan clearly laid out as soon as possible ... a route map that people could buy into internally and externally.[18]

And so, in March 2007, Fox announced a three-year plan for the entertainment retail group that involved a mix of new store formats for HMV, closing some Waterstones stores, taking £40m from the cost base by centralising back office functions and changing the way books get distributed to Waterstones. And naturally, aggressive online growth was part of that plan.

Fox also did something that only a new CEO can do – he admitted the business had failed to rise to the challenges in the market. 'Waterstone's and HMV are great brands,' he said, 'but have not adapted quickly enough to the way customers are buying and consuming media. Our performance has suffered as a consequence.'

The media response was lukewarm at best. *The Times* said: 'HMV's belated digital revolution may be a strategy, but it is not, unfortunately, a solution.'[19] And the *Daily Mail* made him the 'Zero' in their 'Hero and Zero' spot, saying: 'Issuing two profit warnings in four months suggests HMV boss Simon Fox is still struggling to get to grips with market issues. He is facing an uphill task, but his cost cutting plan has done little to inspire faith.'[20]

Two years later the same media trumpeted the great transformation at HMV. For the financial year 2008/09, Fox announced results that showed revenues going back up, and profits up 11.5%. Against the background of a shocking recession, and in a business that can only be described as profoundly structurally challenged, these results were

18 This and subsequent quotes are from interviews with the author.
19 *The Times* (2007) 'Mr Fox – but is he fantastic?' by James Harding, 14 March, http://business.timesonline.co.uk/tol/businesscolumnists/article1512209.ece
20 The *Daily Mail* (2007) 'Hero and Zero', 14 March.

little short of miraculous. Christmas in 2009 delivered another strong set of results for HMV.

The Times ran a glowing profile of Fox in July 2009 headlined: 'HMV and a wily Fox have defied the pundits'.[21] When the UK's main commercial broadcaster ITV was looking for a new chief executive, Fox was said to be the headhunters' favourite because of the turn-around he delivered at HMV. In the end, he withdrew from the process.

As I write this in 2010, HMV is still not home and dry – for reasons I go into below. There are plenty of strategic challenges ahead. But, as we have already seen, the nature of this era of creative disruption is one of continuous challenge, especially for those with their roots in the physical world whose markets have moved online. But Fox took a bad situation and made it better and after speaking to him, and looking at the results, the progress to date offers one of the best blueprints for the often painful process of corporate reinvention.

Lesson 1: Denial, delusion and bewilderment sow the seeds of decline

HMV was a great high street retailer. The business built in the 1970s and 1980s was truly world class. They knew the world of the disc-based music market as well as anyone. But they completely underestimated the impact that the internet was going to have on their markets, and overestimated their capabilities to deal with it and suffered massively as a result.

'There was,' according to Paul Barker who was there at the time, and is now director of communications for HMV Group, 'a general mantra within the business that the internet was only going to be 10% of the music business. The thinking was that mail order had only been 10% so why would this be any different.'[22]

---

21 http://business.timesonline.co.uk/business/industry_sectors/article6624856.ece,
© *The Times* and 02.07.2009/nisyndication.com

22 This and subsequent quotes are from interviews with the author.

As a result, in the first wave of online sales – where the emphasis was on selling CDs – HMV fell behind Amazon. That was unfortunate, but acceptable. But they also fell behind the start-up Play.com, and that should never have happened.

Play.com was launched in 1998 by two entrepreneurs who had been running a sports shop in Jersey, and had taken advantage of the island's tax breaks (no sales tax on any item under £18) to offer cheap merchandise to the UK market over the internet. The best way for HMV to have dealt with this challenger would have been to start doing online fulfilment from the Channel Islands, but they were nervous about cannibalising their store business with cheap business. It took them until 2005 to change their minds, by which time Play.com had built up a loyal customer base. By 2006 Play.com were turning over £250m. Even now, they are ahead of HMV for online CD and DVD sales in the UK.

> **HMV ticked the boxes of digital activity**

HMV ticked the boxes of digital activity. They set up their website. They had kiosks in-store that people could order from. But it was clear they were starting to fall behind in the online world. Simon Fox, explains:

There was a feeling that the internet was not going to be the transformational issue that it's turned out to be, and therefore HMV was not a first mover. So we have been playing catch up for some time, and we let people build up scale businesses while we were still thinking what to do.[23]

Apple launched the iTunes store in June 2004 and it was an immediate success. HMV responded with the launch of HMV Digital, but not until September 2005. It was announced with a great fanfare and the claim they would 'build a market leading digital music player and store that will compete with the best musical software and retail initiatives in the market place'.[24] They didn't.

---

23 This and subsequent quotes are from interviews with the author.
24 From an HMV Strategy presentation in 2005.

HMV had partnered with Microsoft, and the presentation showed an array of not particularly attractive iPod-wannabes from the likes of Creative Audio. HMV's head of e-commerce proudly claimed: 'We don't expect the iPod to retain the market share it has today for very much longer.'[25] But, as we all know, it did.

Yes, such is the benefit of hindsight. However, plenty of businesses misread the music market, just as we saw the executives misreading the encyclopaedia market. It happens. What matters is how you stop it happening in the future.

The mental processes that HMV appears to have gone through was the same that many incumbents experience. First, there is a denial that there is any change happening; next a delusion that because of their brand and the fact that they have always been successful, they are going to be able to be successful here; and finally – when the true horror of the situation starts to emerge – bewilderment sets in.

This was one of the first things Fox had to fix. He describes how he had to change the management mindset (which meant actually changing some of the management) at HMV:

There were some views in the business that were blocking change. There was one kind of school of thought that you just have to keep doing what you always did, and if you kept doing it and just keep doing more of it, things will be ok. And I think there was also a second view which was we are all doomed, and there's not a lot we can do about it.[26]

Lesson 2: Get the core business right first

The headlines that followed Fox's announcement of his strategy were all about the plans to dramatically increase online growth. In fact the results that were applauded two years later came from a much more prosaic programme of improving their physical stores and taking unnecessary cost out of the business. 'Building a large digital business was evidently going to take some time,' Fox says, '[and] we were running out of time in terms of City credibility, and therefore it was extremely important

25 Ibid.
26 From an interview with the author.

to deliver some short-term wins, and visibly be seen to make progress quickly. And so the shorter-term wins which were about revitalising the stores ... were extremely important to buy us time.'[27]

The UK MD of HMV left the business and Fox took on the role himself, cutting out a layer of management and allowing him to focus on fixing the core business. A good signal from the start about where the boss's priorities lay.

The challenge was to ensure that the physical stores still had a role in a world of Amazon, Play.com and iTunes. The stores started to look a bit better. Plasma screens appeared both in the windows and at the gondola ends, and the product mix evolved. Sales of DVDs were already greater than those of CDs, now HMV put greater emphasis on games and technology. Their move into technology was based on an understanding of how people really used their stores. They knew that people often walked into HMV not knowing quite what to buy but wanting to buy *something*. So the technology on their shelves had to be things that people would see and buy there and then, without having to consult anyone else in their household. Headphones, speakers and lots of iPod accessories fitted the bill, but no flat-screen TVs and desktop PCs.

This also meant swallowing their pride and bringing Apple goods into the stores for the first time. 'Apple was the enemy of HMV,' says Fox, 'I thought it should be our friend. It's clearly a brand that consumers love. So why fight these things? You should embrace them. There was resistance, because in one sense Apple are the people that are eating our lunch, so why have them in our stores? The fact is, they're going to eat our lunch whether we sell the produce or not, so we might as well make them our friend.'[28]

As the market contracted, so HMV's rivals fell by the wayside. Tower Records disappeared in 2006. In 2007, the leading independent chain

27 Ibid.
28 Ibid.

Fopp went into administration. In 2008, the Virgin megastore business that had been rebranded Zavvi also folded, as did Woolworths. This gave HMV the chance to boost its share as the last man standing, and improve their high street presence. They acquired Fopp and kept the brand, and in the meantime picked up some of Zavvi's best stores, turning them into HMVs.

With the core business improving, the company no longer needed to load every innovation with the need to turn around the business – as had happened with their digital launch. So they tried a host of new things in store – pay-to-play gaming, a mobile franchise in partnership with Orange and digital cinemas in partnership with the Curzon group. At Christmas they experimented with short-term pop-up stores in areas where there had once been a Zavvi or Woolworths. And when something failed – such as HMV's not very well thought through social network, GetCloser.com, it didn't matter, because the core business looked more robust.

❝ with Waterstones the transformation has been more brutal ❞

With Waterstones the transformation has been more brutal. As well as a shift in the product mix (which has opened them to continuous complaints of 'dumbing down'), they also transformed their distribution system creating a single distribution hub but taking out 300 jobs as a result. This took longer to implement than they had hoped, and Waterstones still faces profound challenges, but its only chance of survival will come from operating with ruthless efficiency.

Lesson 3: Expand the brand: innovate and find adjacencies

If the high street presence was HMV's greatest physical asset, it's greatest intangible asset was its brand. In the early days of denial and delusion, many incumbent businesses place too much faith in how their brand is going to help them transition from one form to the next. Yes, it gives you an advantage, but as the troubles faced in the digital and online market showed it was no guarantee of success.

Marketing director, Graham Sim, carried out extensive work into how far they could take the HMV brand. One visible result of this is that HMV moved from its previous boast of being 'Top dog for music' to 'Get closer'. If you hear any HMV executive speaking now, they will explain that their aim is to 'help our customers get closer to the music, films and games that they love'. At a time when competitive forces are against you, it is vital that the business has a clear function and a role to play in your consumers' lives. Internally and externally, people need to know what your business is there for; and the answer needs to be both credible and positive.

But the work went beyond some rebadging and branding, it also revealed that HMV could take the brand into the world of live music – which unlike recorded music remains a growth market. This led first to a £20m joint venture with Mama Group, which owns a raft of live venues and took on the HMV branding, and ultimately to the purchase of the whole group. In absolute financial terms the deal is marginal (the group had an annual turnover of around £35m, HMV UK alone turns over around £1.1bn), but bolting on a profitable business in a growth market, where your brand and customer relationships can add real value, has to be a good move.

Finally, to 'get closer' to their customers HMV launched a loyalty card, Pure, that allows heavy spenders to get free tickets, signed products and entry to movie premieres.

Lesson 4: You can't do it all on your own

In the end, it proved more worthwhile for HMV to work with Apple than to try and resist them or keep iPods out of their stores on principle. When it came to live music, it took a joint venture with Mama Group to allow them to break into the market. They also worked with the Curzon cinema group in the digital cinema area and trialled a mobile franchise with Orange.

At Waterstones, HMV got behind the Sony e-reader to lead the market – becoming Sony's main retail distribution point. The new distribution centre was outsourced to the logistics firm Unipart. To help with their digital music and e-book infrastructure, HMV also bought a stake in the start-up 7 digital.

It's too simplistic to put these collaborations under the banner of 'partnerships': some of these are straightforward supplier relationships; others acquisitions. But the overall picture is one of greater dependency on the outside world. Incumbent businesses in stable markets become very self-reliant. They think they know best – and within their own world, they very often do. But as the old world becomes less stable and the need to break into new pastures becomes pressing, it makes sense to build on others' experiences and capabilities rather than try and do everything yourself.

Lesson 5 – The process never ends

In a previous era, HMV found a winning formula and stuck to it. With the right management, processes and underlying model in place, it was a case of more and bigger stores leading to more sales and bigger profits. None of that certainty exists any more. There has been an explosion in consumer choice, and the entertainment market is still evolving rapidly. As with all examples of creative disruption: formidable new businesses have been born, while traditional incumbents, HMV and Waterstones among them, have been profoundly challenged.

As a result, HMV – both the core business and the group as a whole – is still not out of the water. For all of Fox's efforts and the fact that he has generally been credited with delivering a remarkable turnaround, the share price at the end of his three-year plan was lower than at the start – a reflection of the long-term, structural weakening of the businesses rather than a reaction to any individual set of results.

Waterstone's profits continue to head in the wrong direction. Even after the cost saving programme and the demise in the UK of Borders, their nearest rival, the business is challenged. HMV have led the way with e-books by working with Sony – but that market is going to escalate dramatically, and they will need to make some bold strategic leaps if they are to compete with Apple, Amazon and Google.

HMV, I suspect, faces interesting times ahead as video and computer games move to downloads. The brutal fact is that after the benefits in market share it has experienced from the decline of its rivals have

❝ you can only change what you can change ❞

started to plateau, it will have to work very hard to secure top-line growth. But, what matters is not a cast iron plan to be able to deal with each and every problem. You can only change what you can change. Fox delivered two things: a focus on making the core business as strong as possible for as long as possible; and a continuous restlessness in the pursuit of new revenue streams and profits. And that is pretty much all you can ask for.

The incumbent's solution: three processes of reinvention

The four businesses we have just looked at had to dig themselves out of trouble. They are very different businesses to what they once were; and the results, in pure financial terms, are mixed. Apple and IBM have gone on to spectacular success – partly because they have managed to position themselves in (or in Apple's case, actually create) markets of high growth. Britannica has got much smaller, but is positioned to start to grow again. HMV has seen its market value decline while it has fought tooth and nail to keep its p&l relatively stable.

Collectively these four provide a fair spectrum of what 'success' looks like, from dramatic growth to survival. Just as importantly, they illustrate what I believe are the three different waves of activity that any business facing creative disruption has to embark upon.

1 Transform the core

The mantra here is to *stick to what you do, but reinvent how you do it*, whether it is IBM reinventing the mainframe, or HMV fixing its stores, or newspapers reinventing their news gathering and production processes for the digital age. The main task for any business facing profound disruption in their core business is not to walk away from it, but to do everything possible to make it fit for the future, satisfying the changing needs of their customers and consumers.

As we will see from a host of examples this means an intertwined programme of innovation and efficiency. If I have become certain of one thing during the writing of this book it is the critical nature of core transformation in the short to medium term.

2 Find big adjacencies

The next thing that has become patently clear is the need to find big adjacent markets if you want to deliver medium- to long-term profitable growth. This is how IBM succeeded, and it is how Apple has ultimately transformed its fortunes. We will see later that this is also how Naspers, the South African newspaper business, has ended up being the largest shareholder in the Chinese social network, Tencent.

Not finding a big adjacency meanwhile is how Britannica ended up so much smaller. I suspect a similar fate will hit many businesses that have specialised in one disrupted business: newspapers and Yellow Pages directories being good examples. If the total revenue in your addressable market is declining, you will ultimately decline with it. The challenge therefore is to move into new markets that either offer growth potential or, at the very least, carry less risk. You are looking for areas where you bring capabilities, scale or customer relationships and insight that can add value; and you also need to believe this can be a big opportunity for you. These are genuine adjacencies, not acts of random diversification.

3 Innovate at the edges

Innovation remains critical throughout – but it has to be focused. It either has to be used to develop the products, services and processes that will help to transform your core business, or it involves taking small steps into what you hope might become big adjacencies. If it doesn't meet one of these two criteria then it will almost certainly be a diversion at a time when you least need to be diverted.

I use the term 'innovation' here to capture a host of different types of activity. It can be an organic development or investment in or acquisition of an innovative and disruptive company in your market. Sometimes it might involve starting something from scratch or taking an undernourished revenue stream from the core business and giving it space to grow.

This process has to take place at the edges of the company. But unless there is a real focus on how you can integrate this into your core offering, or turn it into a scale opportunity, it is no good looking to develop the next big thing and ending up instead with an unmanageable collection of small things.

The benefit of this framework is that it gives structure to any reinvention plan. It should force questions about the balance of activity: are we doing enough to transform our core business? Is this a big adjacency, or just an edge innovation?

As we look at each of these processes in turn, though, it is clear that success is all about execution: what you do, when you do it, and how you do it. The devil, as always, is in the detail. My experience is that for a successful reinvention plan to be put in place, a number of factors – about ownership, management, people and mindset – need to be right within the business. It is also almost inevitable that you are going to have to embark on some process of cannibalisation, or as I euphemistically call it, self-disruption.

" the devil, as always, is in the detail "

If these factors aren't right, and there isn't a smart attitude to cannibalisation, a challenging situation can all too quickly turn into an unwinnable war.

4

The checklist: critical factors for successful reinvention

S uccess within business is all about the decisions you make. But the decisions you make are a subset of the decisions *you are allowed* to make. And what tends to happen is that a number of hard-to-change factors about your organisation limit the decisions people are allowed to make. In that case, it doesn't matter just how capable the individuals within the business might be, they are always going to be operating with at least one arm tied behind their backs.

From my research into reinvention, there are four factors that crop up time and time again:

- the right ownership
- a robust capital structure
- a committed leadership
- the right people: firestarters, rockstars and fixers
- the right mindset: no denial, delusion, distraction or bewilderment.

The right ownership

There is no perfect model for ownership – private, public, family-owned, private equity or non-profit all have their pros and cons.

But, there are good owners and bad owners when it comes to facing disruption within a business and setting about a major transformation programme as a result.

Good owners are prepared to accept that the business they currently own is not the business they once owned, and the business they will own in a few years' time is going to be different again. They are committed to the transformation rather than trying to cling on to the past. This is undeniably difficult for publicly owned companies. When a business faces disruption the 'equity story' – the broad nature of the business's strategic position, financial return, and growth prospects – is changing. This is not welcome news – and it is why no chief executive of a public company can talk about 'structural change' unless they can then back it up with a credible demonstration of what they are going to do about it, and how the shareholders' investments will be protected as a result.

Hence we have seen a dramatic decline in the share prices of traditional media businesses that once benefited from strong barriers to entry, and significant margins as a result. For many, this is likely to have been a permanent recalibration.

Public ownership, then brings its challenges. This is even more true in a post credit-crunch world where the board of directors of public companies do not want to take dramatic risks that could leave them personally liable for shareholders' losses. As one chief executive of a public company I spoke to while researching this book told me: 'I look at my board, and the non-execs that dominate – and I can see it in their faces: they just don't want to take any big risks.'

Bold moves into adjacencies, launches of cannibalistic businesses, and reducing the P&L by launching and running businesses that need to endure a period of loss, are all valid tactics for dealing with disruption; but all very difficult for directors and shareholders of public companies to accept.

This isn't to say that private ownership is always perfect. A private owner might not have access to the funds required to see through a transformation, or might not be able to accept that a business that once effortlessly made money for them has now been transformed into something much, much more challenging. We saw this with Encyclopaedia Britannica which was owned from 1974 by the Benton Foundation. William Benton willed the business to his foundation while it was madly profitable, and it existed primarily as a cash cow to help fund the Foundation's ambitions to ensure that media and telecommunications served the public interest and enhanced democracy.

within a few years, it turned from a cash cow into a loss maker

However, once Britannica suddenly found itself in a knife fight with Microsoft's Encarta, and saw sales and profits start to tumble, it became a very different business. Within a few years, it turned from a cash cow into a loss maker, and a problem. In 1995, the Foundation realised they had to sell it – and so they did, for a price much less than they had hoped, to banker and billionaire, Jacob Safra, who took on the slow and costly task of turning the business round.

How trust ownership helped the Guardian Media Group

The *Guardian* is ultimately owned by the Scott Trust, which was created specifically to ensure the publication of a liberal newspaper in perpetuity. The result is that we don't have shareholders – our job is to fulfil the Trust's remit.

The *Guardian* has to be profit seeking (i.e. it has to be run commercially), but it has been able to afford a loss. Cash to support it is generated from other businesses within the Guardian Media Group, such as Auto Trader or Emap, the business to business publisher.

This ownership has been beneficial at two levels – at a group and a portfolio level. We have been able to buy and sell businesses with relative flexibility to ensure that we have the strongest possible portfolio to generate sufficient cash for the long-term health of the group.

In 2007, for example, we sold half of Auto Trader – an automotive classified business that had done such a brilliant job of transferring to the internet – to the private equity company Apax. A few months later, we again went into joint venture with Apax to buy the business to business wing of Emap plc (events, information services and trade magazines). We also put some cash into an investment fund. The result, we hope, is a balanced portfolio to weather structural change and fund our core purpose: the *Guardian*.

At an operating level, it has also meant we could invest steadily in the *Guardian*'s online efforts – rather than rush in during the dotcom boom and then rush right back out again the second the market turned. The focus has always been on doing the right thing for the long term rather than doing whatever the markets think is right at the time.

During the boom we actually felt profoundly disadvantaged. We had no share options to offer staff. We didn't have access to public markets to make massive investments. It felt like our ownership was actually quite stifling. After the crash, however, we felt profoundly blessed. The fact that we could continue to invest and lead the business to growth and breakeven meant we were in a much stronger competitive position when the market recovered.

Private equity brings with it many positive characteristics for transformation. The business is out of the public's eye, and there is a real focus on turning it round and providing an exit within a challenging timeframe (normally three years or so). Furthermore, management are highly motivated to ensure the business is turned around and has a successful exit – often putting money into the business, with the potential of reaping the rewards if the turnaround goes well.

Those two factors can provide a good environment for the right long-term decisions for transformation. But they don't guarantee it. They can also result in short-term, brutal cost cutting or financial engineering (e.g. sale and leaseback on property portfolios or securitisation of future earnings) – which can improve the short-term flow of cash in the business, and boost the return to the private equity fund's investors, but might not solve underlying problems.

The real problem with private equity though has been debt. They tend to make highly geared acquisitions – which was of no concern when debt markets were free, but left a slew of PE-owned businesses going through the credit crunch constantly having to deal with concerns about their balance sheets, rather than focusing on transforming their business (see below).

The point is that owners – be they public shareholders, private equity, trusts or individuals – all have their advantages and disadvantages as you embark on a process of transformation. They set the expectation for the way that management behaves. If they are not driving change, or at least supporting it, then it isn't going to happen.

Capital structure

If I had been writing this in 2005, this element would have barely made it onto my list. In the early months of 2010 – and after serving two years on the board of a public company – capital structure has to go right to the top. A set of market trends from the past decade have made this one of the toughest to budge features of business around.

Many incumbent businesses – including many newspaper groups and directories businesses, where underlying growth was slowing down – set about delivering growth through consolidation and margin improvement. They went on aggressive, debt-fuelled acquisition drives. This was particularly true after the dotcom collapse when debt was easily available, and it looked, briefly, that a lot of these businesses were not going to be that troubled by the internet after all.

❝ availability of debt fuelled a particular strategic direction ❞

Secondly, private equity came into the market, buying up businesses in need of transformation, again taking on significant levels of debt – 9× EBITDA or more wasn't uncommon – in the hope of sorting the business out and then selling it on, either to a trade buyer or floating it back on to the public market. In both cases, availability of debt fuelled a particular strategic direction.

When the world changed, the lack of debt in the market similarly led to a change in strategy – but probably not in the way that many executive teams would have liked. As the wells of available funds dried up, the acquisitions slowed down, and private equity buyers came out of the market. The fact that there suddenly wasn't a set of buyers in the aisles prepared to pay a premium on the market price for every quoted company going through a bit of difficulty sent share prices down a few notches.

Secondly, companies – both publicly owned and owned by private equity – started to struggle to meet the terms of the debt they had taken on. These are the so-called covenants, which state agreed levels of total debt (normally as a ratio of debt and/or interest payment to EBITDA). Such companies might well be profitable, but as their EBITDAs dropped in the downturn, they found themselves either in breach – or about to breach – their covenants.

So, those companies that have traditionally grown through acquisition and margin improvement found they couldn't grow any more. And, had they wanted to do one of the standard things to boost the balance sheet – sell off non-core businesses – they found that buyers were few and far between. The result was that managing debt – rather than managing a business – became the focus of board activity, taking up massive amounts of time for both the CEO and CFO.

This is a corporate problem on a massive scale. In November 2009, Morgan Stanley predicted that around $3.4 trillion of corporate debt will need to be refinanced over the next five years; the result is going to be thousands of businesses renegotiating their debt. Some might do so by issuing bonds – which effectively just puts the problem back a few years – but even then, the drain on boards will remain significant.

Debt in itself is not a bad thing, but getting on the wrong side of the debt trap is spectacularly stifling for any business, and in particular a business that needs to go through a process of transformation.

The entire corporate focus shifts from long-term goals to ensuring that the covenants are met on a quarterly basis; and any investment that impacts the EBITDA ends up indefinitely delayed. It will also force the sale of profitable businesses that might be able to deliver growth in the future.

While writing this book, I have watched Kodak and Blockbuster both refinance. In the UK media world alone we saw the directories business Yell and two newspaper businesses – Johnston Press and Independent News and Media – all going through the process of very public renegotiations with their banks. At Eniro, the directory business where I sit on the board, we went through a protracted negotiation with the banks that ended in a successful rights issue.

HIT Entertainment, the independent production company, also had to deal with its banks – leaving the fate of children's TV icons such as Thomas the Tank Engine, Bob the Builder and Angelina Ballerina in the balance. We too went through this with Emap: business information group Incisive ended up being 82.5% owned by its banks.

EMI: how debt hurts a turnaround

The most vivid example of how debt can collide with the need for transformation is Terra Firma's £2.4bn acquisition of EMI, which went ahead in July 2007, just before Bear Sterns collapsed and the debt market soon went after it. To secure the deal, Terra Firma lined up £2.6bn of debt from Citi, and invested the maximum amount of their funds they could on an individual deal (30%).

EMI was not in great shape. On the day the deal was announced, they revealed annual losses of £264m, and the shares dropped by 16%. But, a turnaround looked possible. The publishing business (which makes money whenever music is played on air or used by a third party) in particular was very profitable, and the £700m cost base looked very flabby to private equity eyes.

▶

▶

And, as is often the case with private equity, there was a neat bit of financial engineering planned. The commercial viability of the deal was based on the idea of securitisation – taking cash up front based on future earnings. In this case, the plan was to securitise the future cash flows of the music catalogue of older hits. If successful, this would have recouped the entire cost of the acquisition immediately. But this didn't come off. And within 18 months the company was having difficulty meeting its debt covenants. Artists such as Radiohead and the Rolling Stones walked out of the door. There was much public wrangling between Citi and Terra Firma's boss, Guy Hands.

The chief executive, Elio Leoni Sceti, and his management team massively improved the company's financial position. But their ability to invest in new acts and fuel future growth with talent was continuously hampered by the debt issue. In March 2010, Leoni Sceti left the business, to be replaced by former ITV chief executive Charles Allen. More months of wrangling over debt and rumours about what might happen followed, until Terra Firma agreed to put another £105m into the business to stop it being taken over by the banks. Allen himself was then replaced by Roger Faxon, head of EMI Publishing.

There is no elegant solution here. The only strategy to follow is to ensure that the operating business is kept isolated from the debates about funding – even though that can be phenomenally difficult when people are reading about the financial fate of their business in the paper on a daily basis, and noticing cost-cutting measures introduced to ensure that covenants are met.

Leaders committed to transformation

I would never pretend there is an easy time to lead a business, or even that there are businesses that are inherently easy to lead. But there are much, much easier leadership challenges than having to manage any business through a period of profound structural change. The challenge for leaders in this situation is simple to list, but fiendishly difficult to deliver. They have to do four things:

- acknowledge there is a structural problem with the business
- ensure the business comes up with the best possible solution
- ensure it gets delivered
- bring employees and external stakeholders with you throughout the process.

For incumbent leadership teams, the first hurdle is really the hardest and is where many fall. Leaders would not have got to where they are without the ability to lead, to define a plan and to see it followed. They should take 'bringing people with them' as a core part of everything they do. But admitting that the business they have run for a period of years is facing profound change can create dangerously defensive behaviour.

It is at this stage that denial about the severity of the change starts to appear, as does the delusion that either things will soon revert to normal, or that the business is big, strong and successful enough to take this in its stride. The implicit criticism of what has gone before is often too much for some to be able to comprehend, as is the shocking realisation that a huge amount of what they know is increasingly becoming redundant. This is why many business transformations start with the arrival of new leadership to bring a business back from the brink: Gil Amelio, followed by Steve Jobs at Apple; Lou Gerstner arriving at IBM; Simon Fox taking the reins at HMV.

> ❝ a huge amount of what they know is increasingly becoming redundant ❞

But, rather like changing football managers when you have a wave of poor results, this is a drastic measure. And the flip side of this is that you find chief executives who have created a culture of continuous evolution and change will be in their seats for decades: John Chambers at Cisco, Sir Martin Sorrell at WPP, and Koos Bekker at Naspers spring to mind. In all three cases, as we will see when we look at finding big adjacencies, these businesses have delivered sustained growth through ongoing transformation.

Without wishing to sound too sycophantic, I have always admitted that one of the reasons that we as a digital team at the *Guardian* were always capable of doing excellent work was down to supportive and committed leaders – Carolyn McCall as chief executive and Alan Rusbridger as editor-in-chief. Both had their roots in the paper, but both demonstrated unwavering support to the online side of the business. They have always challenged and questioned, but have always supported and shown their external commitment to the development of an industry leading digital business.

When I spoke to my peers at rival newspapers and media companies who talked about endlessly having to explain to their chief executive why they had to have a website, or editors who showed no interest in the online world, I understood that our leadership alone provided us with a significant source of competitive advantage.

The right people: firestarters, rockstars and fixers

It goes without saying that in the toughest of times you need the very best people in the business. For me there are three critical types of people who need to be involved. Not everyone who ends up being critical to your success is going to fit into one of these neat three descriptions – but unless you have these three types you are going to struggle. You need:

- **firestarters** to spark the organisation into action
- **rockstars** that people will follow, and
- **fixers** to make things happen.

They all have a role to play and the best organisations benefit from having a mix of all three.

Firestarters

If you want to get a business to face the fact that it needs radical change you need firestarters to kick the process off. They will not solve your problems for you; their role is to convince the business as a whole that there are massive problems that need to be solved immediately. You might think that mere events can act as a firestarter. A sudden drop in revenues or a big initiative by Google aimed right at your core business should be enough. Sometimes this is the case. The best digital firestarter in most newspaper businesses has been whatever Rupert Murdoch says. Whether it's his moment of 'getting the internet' in 2005, or deciding that 'the internet as we know it is coming to an end' in 2009.

Sometimes firestarters can simply be one or more outside speakers or consultants who can speak to you without the fear of jeopardising their position within the business. Sometimes they can be one or more individuals within an organisation, similar to the loose federation within IBM that drove the internet agenda. Sometimes the CEO or another senior executive can take on the role of firestarter in chief.

The best firestarters will:

- peddle fear and excitement in equal proportion
- speak with authority, ideally as a result of personal experience
- use the right persuasion tactics for the right audience
- speak with sensitivity for the business, but also have the freedom to be blunt without fear of retribution
- provide information and insight, but not necessarily solutions.

Rockstars

When it comes to driving through a programme of radical change within a business, you want a smattering of people that others want to follow; ones who tackle their given field with a certain magic that others can only try to emulate. Rockstars might be leaders – but there may be rock star engineers who would die rather than manage even a couple of people. There is plenty of room for brilliant introverts. Within an organisation there is always

❝ there is plenty of room for brilliant introverts ❞

a tacit, if not explicit, understanding of who the rockstars are. If you see them put on a project, that project suddenly takes on a whole new life. If a CEO says something is really important, but won't put one of his rockstars on the project, then there is always the suspicion that it isn't quite as important to them as they maintain.

In the very early days of the *Guardian*'s website, the editor in chief, Alan Rusbridger, put one of his rockstars in charge of the project – bringing Ian Katz, the then New York correspondent, back to the UK. Ian was acknowledged as one of the paper's rising stars. The message within the business about the importance of the project was clear. Suddenly journalists who had ignored everything we were doing online were suddenly knocking on the door eager to see what we were up to.

The danger with rockstars – especially when they are a big external hire – is that they are not without egos. And for some, their ability to create heat and light and rub people up the wrong way can far outstrip their ability to deliver great products and hit financial targets. Be wary of the big 'rockstar' hire – make sure it's really them you need and not just one of the members of their backing band.

Which is why we need the most unsung and important category of all – the fixers.

Fixers

There are two types of fixers, both equally vital: completer-finishers and peacemakers. They are vital in any organisation at any time, but as you face disruption they become even more important.

My friend Rob Grimshaw, the digital boss at the *Financial Times*, makes the point that traditional media businesses, like many mature organisations, are very silo-based. Year-on-year improvement depends on focusing intensely on operational improvements within these silos. Sales teams sell better; marketing teams focus. But, he points out, as your business starts to transform, chases edge innovations or looks to expand into new areas, you need a very different way of working.

People need to become much more collaborative, you need to bring together all the brainpower in the organisation and get the most out of it. Even a relatively small-scale initiative, such as developing an application for the iPhone, can require input from every function in the business if it is going to be successful.

People say this requires a 'culture of collaboration' – but changing the culture and ways of working within an organisation takes years. What you need are people who can work across traditional boundaries, who can put out the fires that will inevitably start, and who can make things happen. These are the fixers.

Find them. Reward them. Look after them.

The right mindset: no denial, delusion, distraction or bewilderment

Organisations are run by human beings, full of very human emotions. These mindsets provide a challenge for leaders – not least because they might be vulnerable to them themselves. You cannot eradicate them – but you constantly need to be looking out for and dealing with them. Individually and collectively, they are profoundly corrosive.

Denial

In the early days of the internet there was an almost uniform wave of denial about its potential impact among incumbent businesses. It happened in the music industry and it happened in newspapers. It happened at HMV and it happened at Britannica. It happened with the last big technology disruption as well: at IBM in the 1970s no-one thought that PCs would ever provide an alternative to mainframes in any serious business sense.

To those who have denied in the past, I offer complete and utter absolution. It is too easy to snipe with the benefit of hindsight; and I don't think anyone could really have imagined how much the internet would permeate our lives and what the consequences of this would be. Much more has been created, and much more disrupted, than even the most digitally enthusiastic of us imagined.

What we learn from this, though, is that denial – often based on a hunch or what is sometimes referred to as 'Hippo' (the Highest Paid Person's Opinion) – can result in a business. And as we move through 2010, it is vital that there is absolutely no denial that the forces that drive creative disruption are still very active. No business – whether physical or digital – can afford to be complacent as a result.

Delusion

After the acceptance that radical change is under way, delusion sometimes kicks in, and this comes in two forms. First is the delusion about your position in the old world. Second comes the delusion about your potential in the new world.

Incumbent businesses have significant assets that they can carry through the process of reinvention and these provide them with advantage. Strong brands, customer relationships and insight, and economic scale are those that go to the top of most incumbents' lists. All valid, but they are a source of advantage, not a guarantee of it. They will prove of only limited advantage if someone provides a product that offers a similar service to you, but at 20% of the cost, or for free. This is why I stress that one of the first challenges for transforming the core of your business is to challenge all the assumptions you have about your customers, consumers and competition. Take nothing for granted.

❝ take nothing for granted ❞

The next delusion is that your new intiatives are, on their own, going to save the day. In other words – pure growth, digital or otherwise, is going to save the need for the more challenging world of cost reduction, tightening up processes and sorting out efficiencies.

Just as the early days of the internet saw denial of its impact, it also saw some delusions about the money that many businesses could make – and some silly levels of investment as a result. In 2010, however, there is too much hard data to make those mistakes again.

Be honest about your flaws. Be honest about your potential. Act accordingly.

Distraction

Again, there are two types of distraction: the old world stops you focusing on the new; or the new world stops you focusing on the old. One of the characteristics of disrupted and declining markets is ferocious fights for market share. It's the best source of growth in the circumstances.

As we will see in Chapter 8, Kodak's immediate challenge in the late 1990s was not the arrival of digital imagery – that would only make a financial impact years later – it was the arrival of cheap film from around the world, and in particular a price war with Fuji. At the time, billions in film sales rested on the outcome. A decade later, however, and those billions simply don't exist any more.

Similarly, in the UK newspaper market between 2003 and 2005, all anyone could talk about was what format their newspapers should adopt. The *Independent* went tabloid and gained some circulation. *The Times* followed. The *Guardian* followed its own path and took on a Berliner format. At the time, I sat on the board of the *Guardian* and format dominated discussion, month in month out.

These are real problems that need focus and solutions. Get them wrong, and you might not have a future to worry about. But to stop investing, testing and trialling the products and services that will be your future, is a potentially fatal flaw.

Similarly, it is all too easy for executives constantly in pursuit of the next new thing to let the traditional business slip. In Chapter 9, I talk about how critical it is for book publishers to get the right terms in place with Google, Apple and Amazon to ensure they have the basis for a successful digital future. However, if they do this at the expense of bringing out the very best physical books, as efficiently as possible, and competing as ferociously as they always have done, then there will not be much of a business to build a digital future on.

This need for a real focus on both the old and the new is critical but difficult to pull off. A look back over the agendas for the last year's executive and board meetings, and discussions at off-sites, should give some indication of whether you are getting the balance right. If you're not – do something about it: now.

Bewilderment

This tends to happen in businesses where success and growth has been a way of life: a natural consequence of being in the right market, at the right time and operating in the right way. When this perfect alignment of stars breaks down the result is often bewilderment. This is exactly what Simon Fox described at HMV when he said he found people thinking: 'We are all doomed, and there's not a lot we can do about it.'[1]

A once focused organisation suddenly becomes a mix of headless chickens and rabbits caught in the headlights – especially, as we will see, when a big decision has to be made that will potentially cannibalise your core business.

One of the first things many traumatised and bewildered incumbents do is head to regulators hoping for protection. In the case of Kodak and Fuji, Kodak took the case to the World Trade Organization, and lost. Personally, I have spent countless hours over the years complaining about the BBC or Google to various regulators. Sometimes it has been constructive; but looking back much of the activity proved to be massively diversionary. The corridors of power are long and winding – it's very easy to get lost in there.

---

1 In interview with the author.

Leadership here is critical. It's not about making reckless promises about the future, or Churchillian speeches – it is about defining the most important things that you can do and making sure they get done. It's about realising that in really challenging times there is no good solution; the least worst solution is the best you will get. Above all, it means not trying to change things you have no control over.

The 'C' word: taking a smart approach to cannibalisation

The final factor for success really deserves a chapter on its own: taking a smart approach to cannibalisation.

I don't really like the term cannibalisation. It shifts you back to thinking protectively about the past rather than progressively about the future. But I know that in businesses around the world faced with the internet, the 'C' word crops up, and the fear about it can leave you paralysed. It is profoundly counter-intuitive to launch a new business that could kill your existing one.

The brutal refrain is that 'you should eat your babies before someone else does', and there is some point in this. As I have analysed one business after another in putting this book together, I haven't found a single example where a business has managed to reverse the process of creative disruption and save itself by refusing to cannibalise itself. Kodak didn't stop the rise of digital photography by being cautious about cannibalising its film business. HMV didn't protect its stores by refusing to sell cheap CDs online, it simply allowed Play.com to steal a march. Britannica didn't save its encyclopaedias by pricing its CD-roms at the same price as its print products.

At the same time, successful reinvention has more often than not come from some degree of cannibalisation. In the newspaper world, one of the groups that is generally deemed to have done the best job in the face of creative disruption has been the Norwegian newspaper

> **❝ successful reinvention has more often than not come from some degree of cannibalisation ❞**

group Schibsted. It has cannibalised itself by launching and acquiring a raft of online-only classified sites that are allowed to compete with its newspapers. These online classified sites now account for approximately 40% of group profits, with an operating margin of 25% as opposed to the 8–10% margins on their traditional business. And, we will see at the end of this chapter how Auto Trader and Getty Images have both similarly cannibalised themselves – and become stronger as a result.

Cannibalisation is not something you would choose to do – but it is something you have to tackle if you want to continue to meet your customers' needs in a changing world. If you fail to do that, you won't have protected your business – you will have killed it.

The fear of cannibalisation is as dangerous as cannibalisation itself

For newspapers, one of the great challenges of cannibalisation concerns classified advertising. Should we allow our clients to buy advertising online-only, much cheaper? To advertise a job in print costs around £1,000; to advertise the same job online only costs a maximum of £300. This was something we debated, literally for years, until a consultant came in who had previously worked in an online jobsite. 'We know we can sell against you, because we know you're worried about cannibalising your print sales,'[2] he pointed out when we met. And he was right.

We started to offer online-only advertising everywhere as a result of this meeting and after a number of conversations with our customers. The consequence was that our online revenues soared. Our print revenues have continued to decline – but this is in line with the market. We thought we were protecting our revenues, instead we were failing to meet our customers' needs and allowing competitors to grow as a result. When I've spoken to entrepreneurs and venture

---

2 In a meeting with the author.

capitalists, they are all too aware that an incumbent's inability or unwillingness to cannibalise themselves can give new entrants a significant advantage.

Saul Klein, now a partner with Index Venture Capital in London, was one of the founders of Video Island, which took the Netflix model over to the UK (it later merged with LOVEFiLM). 'We knew that our proposition of 'no late fees' was just great for consumers, it was something Blockbuster just couldn't compete with, because late fees accounted for a significant part of their profits,'[3] he said. The result was that Blockbuster ultimately had to drop its late fees policy, but only after Netflix and LOVEFiLM took control of the mail-order video rental market.

Another venture capitalist I spoke to gave me a general rule of thumb: if an entrepreneur is going to make a disruptive launch against an incumbent, they can normally count on the fact that they'll have two or three years to build their business up, before the incumbent will be willing to cannibalise itself and compete. This is a double whammy for the incumbent. First, you have to say goodbye to the barriers to entry that have protected you for so long. Next, you are letting the new entrant create barriers to entry around themselves, because they know you can't compete with them head on for fear of cannibalisation.

It's not whether you do it, but how and where you do it

But simply blundering in, 'eating your babies' and hoping you will solve all your problems can be as flawed as doing nothing. The trick is all about how, when and where you do it.

There is a real danger when you cannibalise a strong business with a commodity business. This is what happened to Kodak when they started to move from consumer film imaging to consumer digital imaging. It meant a move from a profitable business with high barriers

---

3 In interview with the author.

to entry to a loss-making business with a raft of competitors. They had to do it, and it may ultimately reap dividends, but the real growth potential – and what margins they have – come by using the remnants of their film and chemicals division to generate cash, and moving into the big adjacency of digitised professional printing.

IBM's most simple cannibalistic response to PCs disrupting the mainframe market was to cannibalise themselves by selling PCs, which it did. But PCs rapidly became a commodity market – so IBM got out of it. Their move into services – which as we have seen ultimately saved IBM – was equally cannibalistic, although not as obviously so. IBM's services team would infuriate the hardware sales team by recommending that companies buy non-IBM hardware and software. In his memoir, Lou Gerstner commented that he would have to deal with a fight between the hardware sales teams and his services team nearly every week. But services was a growth area with good margins: unlike the PC market it was well worth the disruption.

Timing, positioning and managing of cannibalisation is a delicate skill. This is why you need to put all your efforts into thinking how you're going to do it, rather than getting caught in the corporate ping-pong debate of 'should we do it or shouldn't we?'

The $19bn bet: cannibalising Microsoft Office

Microsoft faces a massive disruption around its Office business as a result of web-based applications, predominately Google's suite of applications. Office accounts for about 90% of Microsoft's $19bn Business Division, and they are going to be very careful about doing anything that destabilises that business any quicker than they have to. But, if they refuse to meet the rise of free hosted applications head on, they will find their role on desktops around the world increasingly diminished. Microsoft is fighting this on two fronts. First, the 'Home and Student' edition of Office is getting cheaper, but with Office 2010, they are making a free version of the key Office apps available online.

Is this free version a great idea or a dumb one? Holding back would have been dumb, but the ultimate success will be all about execution: the mix of features between free and paid-for, and the comparison with Google apps. One important aspect is that a free online version might help with the other great disruptive force in Microsoft's sector: piracy in developing economies. Above all, the longer they can keep people away from using Google Apps, and keep them within the Microsoft world – even if it is for free – the healthier their business has to be.

None of this takes away the need to keep improving their core Office product. Microsoft have to provide reasons for businesses and consumers to upgrade to Office 2010 and beyond; increasingly ensuring that trial versions come installed on new PCs and laptops that can be activated online, thus saving on the cost of manufacturing and distributing discs.

I now want to focus on two very different cases of successful cannibalisation – the first being the organic development at Auto Trader in the UK, which I believe is one of the most successful transformations from print to digital anywhere in the world. The second is cannibalisation by acquisition, which looks at the success of Getty Images' purchase of iStockPhoto.

Auto Trader: growth through organic cannibalisation

Auto Trader in the UK was a publishing phenomenon. Launched in the 1970s in the UK it hoovered up car classifieds from the regional press and became massively profitable. By the early 1990s there were actually two different businesses operating under the *Auto Trader* banner in different parts of the UK. And thanks to a bit of consolidation in 1998, the Guardian Media Group owned 48% of it in partnership with the private equity firm, BC Partners.

At the time, the magazine's national circulation was around 350,000. If you were buying or selling a car, you bought a copy of your local *Auto Trader*. The internet, however, threatened to change all of that.

&&the internet was just a thing for geeks at the time 55

Graham Luff, then the chief executive of the newly formed Trader Media Group, had seen the internet coming – and been swift to acknowledge the impact it was going to have on his business. In truth, the management team knew this technology had the potential to seriously damage their print product. What should they do? They were clear market leaders. The internet was just a thing for geeks at the time. Maybe they should launch a website, but did they really have to take it seriously?

Well, they did. They launched onto the internet with full gusto. They didn't just build a website, but they built a separate business which set out to directly challenge their print business, with different sales teams who would actively (and sometimes it has to be admitted, counter-productively) sold against each other. They also did something which seemed way, way beyond their capabilities at the time, developing a software package called Dealer Edit, which allowed dealers to manage the stock on their forecourts – and then by pressing a few buttons, to send advertising straight to the Autotrader.co.uk website.

At the time of writing, *Auto Trader*'s print circulation is now around 100,000. About 50% of its revenues come from the web but, importantly, about 80% of its profits. Over this period it has achieved that rarest of phenomena – increased profitability from its a complete move to digital. It has not been easy, however. There has been ferocious competition along the way – including a full-on assault from eBay. There has also been wave after wave of cost cutting as the print business has gone into decline.

Real success has come from excellent execution over more than a decade, making sure that *Auto Trader* continues to succeed in the digital world as they once did in print by offering car dealers and car buyers the best marketplace out there. The point is that you can only have such focus, and deliver effectively, if you are not continuously having to fight internal battles around the 'C' word.

Even now, the digital team has to innovate to keep ahead, and has to work hard for growth. Relations between the print and web teams have not always been harmonious – particularly in the early days. But at no point have they wavered from delivering a strong profitable business via whichever channel the market wants.

Getty Images: from stock to microstock – cannibalisation through acquisition

Getty Images was launched in the mid 1990s by Mark Getty and his partner Jonathan Klein. They consolidated and digitised what had been a very fragmented market of stock photography agencies, buying up business after business, taking out cost, making their core database stronger and expanding their customer base along the way.

The internet was a phenomenal enabling technology to this sector. It allowed the business to service customers much, much more cheaply and effectively than previously, and Getty reaped the rewards of this. They consolidated and dominated the market, with nearly three times the revenues of their nearest competitor, Corbis, founded by Microsoft's Bill Gates.

The great challenge, however, came from a new world, of what was called Microstock photography. Rather than paying hundreds of dollars for an image by a select number of photographers at Getty or Corbis, they can visit a site such as iStockPhoto and pay cents or perhaps a few dollars at most for an image that would have been put up there by photographers who, in all probability, wouldn't have been allowed to have their work in one of the established stock collection.

Microstock businesses expanded the market. Thousands of previously amateur photographers were able to sell their work, and a whole load of new customers came into the market. In one analysis from Getty, 50% of Microstock customers had never used a stock agency before. For the big stock libraries this was a problem. At a Corbis management meeting, Bill Gates asked: 'Why would anyone pay $200 for a picture of a bear if they could get one for a dollar?'[4]

4 Quoted in Business 2.0 on 1 April 2007 at http://money.cnn.com/magazines/business2/business2_archive/2007/04/01/8403372/index.htm

For Getty there were three options. They could ignore the new sector; they could launch 'Getty lite'; or they could buy their way into the market. The first option would have been an act of denial bordering on negligence. The second one, given the assets they had at their disposal, would have been theoretically possible, but they would have found themselves competing against a host of other businesses who only operated at this end of the business, and they would always be playing catch up. Furthermore, this was a business based on growth through acquisition, why should they behave differently now?

So, in the end, Getty chose the last option and, in 2006, bought iStockPhoto, the microstock market leader, for a rumoured $50m. By 2009, iStock's executives were talking about doing some $200m in revenues – that would have made them about a quarter of Getty's business. Getty was bought by private equity in 2008 at a value of around $2.4bn, so you get a sense that iStock is now considerably more than the money Getty paid for it.

the rules of engagement are clear

What's important is that while Getty rebranded pretty much every business it bought, when it bought iStockPhoto, it allowed the business to keep its own branding. But, they have enhanced the service using Getty's own taxonomy. In other words, the rules of engagement are clear: use Getty's capabilities to help differentiate it from the hundreds of other microstock sites now out there, but it has to remain part of the microstock world.

Getty still has to fight hard to keep its core business – it still needs to keep 75% of its revenues in as healthy a state as possible for as long as possible. But, increasingly, a large army of customers' needs will be met through microstock photography. It is a growth business, and thanks to Getty's cannibalistic acquisition, they own the market leader.

5

Transform the core

reative disruption weakens incumbents. As we have seen it has three main impacts.

- As traditional sources of competitive advantage – such as high barriers to entry – are weakened, your core business will no longer be as structurally secure as it was.

- As technology advances, and you have to evolve your business to meet changing consumer wants and needs, and you will find many of your old 'ways of doing things' are no longer optimal (as Schumpeter would have put it).

- As a direct result of the two factors above – potentially compounded by broader economic upheaval – you will suffer at best margin erosion, at worst a significant fall in your top and bottom lines. Either way your financial position will no longer be as strong as it once was.

These factors combined mean that your business is going to have lower growth prospects than previously, and face greater competitive pressure. From the detached view of an investor, the business is no longer as good a bet as it once was. But, even when all of this is true, it doesn't mean that there is no longer a business there – it simply means that the business is going to have to face up to a process of radical reinvention.

As we will see in the next chapter, real growth is very possibly going to have to come from moving into new adjacencies. But, your core business – for all of its new-found frailty – is still going to be where your greatest assets and your greatest liabilities lie. It will almost certainly be your greatest source of revenue and profit. Should you lose focus on it for a second, or should you think that it can somehow continue as it once did, then your chances of being able to move into new growth areas will be severely restricted.

If I have become convinced of one thing during the researching and writing of this book it is the importance of core transformation. In the box below I give five reasons why it is so vital.

Five reasons why transforming the core must be your priority

1 The big thing is that the big thing, is the big thing

Your core business is where the vast majority of your assets and your liabilities lie. It generates the most revenue and it carries the most cost. Slips or gains here will have a greater impact on your business as a whole. It might need reinventing and dramatic change – but it cannot be ignored.

2 A sound core provides the best possible base for innovation and expansion

If your core business is in decline, or facing dramatic upheaval, the ultimate strategic solution is very probably going to have to come from finding new areas. But, if you do this from a weak core, you will find yourself constantly having to come back to fix it. Deutsche Post and Nokia (see below) provide examples of what happens when you do, and don't, take this on board.

3 Rumours of 'death' are often over-exaggerated

We still buy newspapers and CDs. We go into travel agents on the high street, and we buy. We buy physical books to read on holiday. All of these behaviours may be in long-term decline as a result of creative disruption – but they are a long, long way from dead. No-one in these businesses can walk away from these 'old ways of doing things' for some time yet.

4 Sometimes your core will be all you have

It is great to think you might be able to move into a big new adjacency and find a new stream of growth. But very often, that can't happen. Either there is no opportunity there, or your owner or shareholders don't think it is the best use of their money for you to pursue it.

5 Core transformation is a long, hard slog: best to start early, then

Bringing about radical change in a business is no small matter, especially if it is a business that has essentially created one thing in one way for as long as anyone can remember. It means changing people, processes and mindsets. The sooner you start, the longer you will have to get it right.

The transformation challenge for record labels

Record labels provide a good example of the need for transformation at the core of the business. There are few businesses that have been as structurally challenged as they have. How much their fate is a consequence of their own actions, and how much is simply the gravity of disruption, is neither here nor there; but the brutal truth is that the value of their core business – the sale of recorded music – has fallen by billions over the past decade. That money has gone: it is not coming back. But the *function* of their core business – of finding talent, developing it, and commercially benefiting from the results of it – is still very valid.

The slump in the size of their market has made running a label in 2010 a much tougher job than it was in 1990. So has the arrival of new competition: Live Nation, Starbucks and a host of others have started to compete with labels, and many more will follow. But the majority of the world's biggest acts are signed to one of the major labels; and most of the world's up-and-coming acts hope that they will be one day.

Furthermore, despite the decline in recorded music revenues – it was still a global market worth more than $17bn a year in 2009.[1] The prize of discovering the next Coldplay or Britney is well worth fighting for. In fact, it has become even more worth fighting for than before, because sales of the biggest hits are holding up best. Essentially it's better to have one act in the top tier than half a dozen in the tier below.

There has been a shift in value towards live music – where labels haven't traditionally generated revenue – but this has brought it onto a par with recorded music, rather than dwarfed it. According to figures compiled by the collections agency, PRS for Music, the value of live music in the UK in 2008 rose by 13% to £1.39bn only marginally ahead of recorded revenues of £1.3bn.[2] So yes, live music is growing, but recorded music is still a large part of the overall pie – and within that sales of good old fashioned CDs still provide a large part of the value.

❝ labels need to build on successful relationships ❞ For long-term growth, labels need to build on successful relationships around recorded music and move into other revenue areas such as live music: so-called '360 degree deals'. But the key phrase there is 'successful relationships'. They're not going to be able to do this unless they reinvent their recorded music business to appeal to the world we now find ourselves in.

The logic here is simple and very human. If you are a successful artist and your label can't help a band through the recording and release process, or provide the best possible marketing support, as well as providing the human support when things aren't going as well as they might, then why would you let them manage your live performances or take a slice of your merchandising sales?

---

1 IFPI, www.ifpi.org
2 Will Page (2008) 'Adding up the Music Industry for 2008', *PRS for Music*, www.prsformusic.com/economics

As John Reid, the CEO of Warner Music Europe has said:

Always focus on the artist, it's about the artist and the record, if you do that, then we're fine. With most artists, what they want to know is that their guy in the record company is there for them. Your A&R person is your champion. Navigating the creative relationship is the hardest thing in music but the most important.[3]

The difference though is that the reduction in recorded music revenues means labels are changing the way they do business. At one level this means reducing the number of loss-making artists on their roster. It also means using much smarter marketing solutions: making greater use of the web and social media, as well as direct contact with fans through CRM databases.

It has also meant constant tweaking of pricing and products – hence the fact that every new release now comes in its basic version, but also a host of premium offerings, both physical and digital. The challenge is to keep the entry price for legal music – whether physical or digital – low enough to keep some fans away from piracy, but also to tap into others' willingness to pay whatever it takes to have the latest offering from their favourite artist.

In terms of financial management, it also means a much greater focus throughout the business on margins rather than volumes. In the old days of selling CDs at a fixed price, margin was a by-product of volume; but in this world of multiple products, channels and price points it is all too easy to see volumes soar and profits tumble.

Those running labels are all too aware of the need to focus on this process of reinvention. Ged Doherty, who took over as chair of Sony BMG in the UK in 2005, said he 'hated' the first six months of his job, 'I wasn't sure whether to focus on the music, the internet, the legislation … once I decided to focus on music, then everything else took

---

3 *Observer Music Monthly*, February 2008, http://www.guardian.co.uk/music/musicblog/2008/feb/02/thefutureofmusic/

care of itself.'[4] He set an ambitious target to break five new acts – and in the end they broke seven.

There is nothing radical in that ambition. But the business that delivered that very traditional goal was undergoing radical change. Nearly a third of the staff left. Half of the new people Doherty brought into the business came from outside the music industry. He increased the size of the customer insight unit and brought in the futurist Gerd Leonhard as a consultant for a year (a classic 'Firestarter' move). Marketing techniques that had been used for decades started to change. For the release of Dido's album *Safe Trip Home*, the label commissioned 12 short films that were seeded online, rather than simply resorting to the traditional mix of TV, press and poster advertising. There was also the inevitable clampdown on cost: at one point Doherty sent round a memo saying that he would personally sign off all taxi receipts: the bill fell instantly by 80%.

For many of those working in the business at the time, this was not a great period. This kind of change involves a world of pain but it is, unfortunately, necessary. If labels have a future, they will have it because they stuck to what they do best, but reinvented how they do it, and then build out from this strengthened core business. That is the task for disrupted incumbents everywhere.

Stick to what you do – reinvent how you do it

This then is our challenge – to take the core business and make it relevant for the new world we find ourselves in. It is what Simon Fox had to do when he set about transforming HMV's stores; what Lou Gerstner did when he invested in CMOS technology that allowed IBM to resuscitate the mainframe business; and it is what Steve Jobs did at Apple when he sorted out the supply chain, cut the number of products Apple was producing and brought the company back to profitability before delivering the iMac, iPod and iPhone that redefined consumer electronics.

---

4 Ibid.

This process of core transformation builds mostly on good business practice – particularly the tried and tested methods of change management that are well documented in a range of business books and articles.[5]

I want to highlight seven critical factors in any successful transformation:

1 Challenge all your assumptions about your customers and consumers.

2 Define what your core is and what it's going to be.

3 Identify the four different types of core activity.

4 Look after your brand and it will look after you.

5 Don't be proud: pinch ideas from your disruptors.

6 Bring people with you.

7 Structure your business to reflect what's core and what's edge.

1 Challenge all your assumptions about your customers and consumers

As we said at the outset, technology enables change – but people make it happen. The reason your core business is challenged is ultimately because of the changing behaviour of your customers and consumers. Patterns of behaviour that might have been stable for decades – handed down from generation to generation – such as buying a physical version of recorded music, or buying and reading a newspaper in the morning – have shifted, and the businesses that prospered from these behaviours have suffered as a result.

This puts an unprecedented burden on businesses to challenge all their assumptions and understandings about their customers and consumers,

5 The essential starting point is John Kotter's *Why Transformation Efforts Fail*, http://hbr.org/product/leading-change-why-transformation-efforts-fail-hbr/an/R0701J-PDF-ENG

> **" the wrong starting assumption can set you back by years "**

and how they spend their time and money. Getting this right is critical. Your assumptions about your market and about your customers and consumers are a vital building block as you start to plot for the future. Any strategy document or plan should start with those basic assumptions. If they prove to be wrong, it's very likely you will need to change your strategy. As we saw when HMV predicted that the internet would amount to only 10% of the music industry, the wrong starting assumption can set you back by years.

This is not a one-off process or a single piece of research. This is about a change in your behaviour – in three ways:

- **Gather more information.** If you don't have a customer panel, start one. If you do, make it bigger – tap into it more often. If you regularly hold focus groups, hold more. Look at all the data sources coming into your business. Don't just focus on your traditional competitive set – get under the skin of everyone who is trying to steal your lunch.

- **Provide better insight.** Data without insight is a wasted resource. Insight locked within a small number of people in the business is equally useless. Make sure you have people with the skills to provide insight from this deluge of information; make sure it spreads through the business – communicate it, provide dashboards and make sure people are using it.

- **Cut the hunch quota.** There will always be decisions made by hunch within any business. Long may it last. But, hunches need to come with a health warning – just because something sounds plausible and/or exciting, doesn't make it true. You need to be equally wary of hunches and insight based on a previous era, and of grand tech-fuelled pronouncements about how the world has changed.

2   Define what your core is and what it's going to be

It is not enough to talk about transformation – you have to be clear about what you are transforming yourself from and into. This happens at two levels: the first is the headline level of defining yourself by what you do, rather than where you do it or how you do it. This is what Tom Glocer, CEO of Reuters, has described as 'abstracting yourself away from the distribution mechanism of the day, and working out what it is you really do'.[6]

At its most superficial level, this is by now the well-worn process of, for example, a newspaper business describing themselves as a news business. Likewise, a Yellow Pages business will start to talk about the role of bringing buyers and sellers together. Anyone can do this. The real challenge, though, is whether you mean it, believe it and you're prepared to act on it.

There are, for example, two types of traditional retailers who go online. There are retailers with shops and websites that might carry the same brand and much of the same stock, and who might call themselves 'multichannel retailers'; and there are true multichannel retailers, who use both physical stores and an online presence, separately and in conjunction, to build a stronger, overall retail business.

A good example is Argos in the UK, a general interest store selling everything from jewellery to tents to iPods. No stock is on display and everything is ordered through catalogues at the front of the store. Online, they would be nothing more than Amazon without the books and DVDs. On the high street alone, they are a throwback to a previous era. But combining mobile, online and the high street locations they have been transformed. Being able to go online and see which Argos store has exactly what you want in stock, then click and reserve it and go and collect it within minutes has dramatically improved the overall quality of what they offer consumers.

6 Speaking on stage at DLD 2010, Hamburg, February 2010.

This difference between just talking about reinvention and delivery is why the next part of the process is so vital. The challenge is never about creating ideas; it is about making them happen.

In the following box I've suggested two exercises that I have found useful to help with this process: 'future retrospectives' and 'from-and-to grids'. They are a complement to the sort of strategic analysis you would normally go through – but they are both good ways to start to make the change feel very real to people. Both can be used at different levels throughout the business, both spark debate and both start to rapidly move us from a world of bold strategic statements to tangible changes in what people do day to day.

People need to know the destination they are heading for. They need to feel motivated by ambitious but realistic targets. For most people in the business this will mean concrete 'from and tos' rather than bold abstracts. At the Guardian, one of the great breakthroughs in the early days of our online recruitment operation – when monthly revenues were around £200–300K – was to stop talking about high-level strategy and new product ideas, and instead get everyone to focus on what it would take to deliver £1m revenue a month. Within minutes sales managers who had been sitting with their arms crossed were fighting to get up to the whiteboard to detail what it would take, and what we needed to do to get there. We delivered the '£1m a month' 18 months later.

Two exercises in defining your future

The future retrospective

Write an article about your transformation for an edition of the *Wall Street Journal*, *Financial Times* or your own specialist magazine or blog, but imagine it in three or five years' time. This should be between 500–1,500 words long – long enough to demand a fair amount of detail to be crammed in. While the priority is to create something readable and hopefully entertaining, it needs to be grounded in fact. You need to be prepared to back up your predictions about the change both within your business, and around it, with some form of evidence.

You can ask a group to do individual versions of these, and then distributing them in advance to use as material for a discussion/ workshop is a great way to drive out areas of agreement, disagreement and uncertainty.

The from-and-to grid

The next step is to distil this work into a 'from-and-to grid' such as that shown below.

	From	To
External factors		
Customers/consumers		
Competitors		
Internal factors		
Processes		
Systems		
Skills		
Outputs		
Products		
Financials		

The categories down the left-hand side are just for guidance – and they should have further breakdowns. It may be that you need to specify individual processes or systems. You might want to separate consumer or customer behaviour according to the description of the changing make-up of your customer/consumer base.

If you want to make it even more intricate you can add extra columns with different time horizons (e.g. 1, 3 and 5 years) to add a greater sense of the breakdown of how transformation within your business is going to happen.

3 Identify the four different types of core activity

As the picture of how your business is going to look starts to emerge the next challenge is how you get there. Very broadly, you should start to develop a sense of four elements or types of activity within the core business:

1 **Things we do now that we will still do in the future.** Even through all of this turmoil there are going to remain many things that you do now that you will do in the future. The focus here is how can we do this better, and ideally, more efficiently? How can we use technology to help us? In newspapers, this is all about the core process of gathering news, and producing content. We do it now, we will do it in five, ten and probably 20 years' time: the challenge is how we do it smarter; how we use the web, mobile and social media to help develop, build and distribute our stories; as well as making sure we have the right systems in place to ensure that news ends up in the right place at the right time.

2 **Things we don't do now we'll need to do in the future.** As it becomes clear that you need to build new skills and develop new products and processes, the task here is to start to experiment and learn as soon as is possible. This is one of the areas that we'll look at later – 'edge innovations' – developing the next wave of core activity away from the core to give the former space to develop. Again, from my experience in newspapers, this is where much activity with video has lived.

3 **Things we do now we won't do in the future.** The toughest and most important decisions you will make are about what you will stop doing. This is the brutal part of your new reality: something has to give. The idea of doing 'more with less' is optimistic at best, and the road to exhaustion, frustration and bewilderment at worst. There may be things that can be stopped immediately; others will have some months or years left in them yet. The tasks here are simple: first you have to ensure that this activity is as lean as it can be. Next you have to agree the triggers that will

lead to it being stopped – and ensure that the right processes and systems are in place for this to be monitored.

4 **Things we do now, that aren't really 'core' but have growth potential.** Sometimes there are revenue streams or products that are good ideas with potential, but either they can't get the attention they need to grow while they sit in the core business, or they may get too much attention – and become a diversion away from the core. Here the equation is simple: if you think it has the potential to be a big adjacency then you make it an 'edge innovation' and build it up. If you don't, it has to be stopped (see above). At the Guardian we noticed that we had a number of events and supplements that sat in different places all aimed at the public sector market – many as marketing activity to support our recruitment advertising business. After some experimentation, we put all of this into a single business unit, called Guardian Professional, that it is now a significant profit contributor to the company.

My suggestion is to get all of this onto one sheet of paper – and look at the comparative size of the lists.

What's important is the balance in the size of the columns. If you're starting more than you're stopping – you have a problem. If you're not starting enough new things – you have a problem. If you don't have any fledgling businesses that can be developed into meaningful revenue streams, then you are going to have to look very hard for new adjacencies if you want to see any growth in the future.

4 Look after your brand and it will look after you

If there is one key advantage that incumbent businesses have, it is their brands. Start-ups might be nimble, they might live and breathe the internet, and they might have a host of things in their favour as they march into the world – but building a real brand takes time, and many of them fail.

Then again, if there is one disadvantage that incumbent businesses have, it is in believing that the historic strength of their brands somehow gives them an entitlement to success as they set about transforming their business.

There was nothing wrong with the Polaroid brand, for example, but as a business they failed to move on when digital technology left the world of instant. As we will see when we look at Kodak, they had a brilliant brand in many ways – but it didn't protect them from a price war with Fuji in the late 1990s, and then stop their consumers shifting to digital a few years later.

When a business goes through the sort of core transformation that we are discussing, it is like the human body going through growth: nearly every molecule gets changed. Your brand, however, like the human personality is one of the few constants throughout this change.

The process of 'looking after your brand' in the online world is not simply a matter of spending money on TV ads to give people a warm, fuzzy feeling about your business. It is about ensuring that your business continues to seem relevant and continues to live up to the values that you ascribe to your brand – and that you hope that customers and consumers ascribe to you too. It is about smart management of your reputation in a world of blogs and tweets and Facebook groups. It is about making sure that everything you are doing – from call centre conversations to corporate brochures – is true to your brand.

> **❝ it is about making sure that everything you are doing is true to your brand ❞**

The reason is that your brand is not just a defensive barrier for your core business but a platform to help you migrate into new areas. HMV's move into technology and live music; IBM's move into services; Apple's move into MP3 players – all of these came from extending brands that had potential way beyond their traditional heartland. In all three cases, these moves were preceded by strong brand advertising; and in all cases, I suspect that both the advertising and the moves into adjacencies stemmed from a powerful understanding of the brands' strengths and potential in a changing world.

Very often businesses create new brands to break out into new ventures. I am deeply suspicious of this as an opening gambit into the new world. In the short term it gives you a bit of speed, and frees you from the shackles of your core brand. But in the long term it often proves to be a diversion. Retail banks which had quite stuffy images were all very keen on this during the dotcom boom – spinning off funky little internet businesses in the time it would normally have taken their core business to make a decision over office furniture. Abbey National's launch of Cahoot was a good example.

The problem is that after the intial euphoria, you are still left having to build an online presence for your core business; and you now have a second brand to support. After a while these new brands tend to be sold off, spun back into the core, or simply hover in the limbo of marginal profitability, making a contribution that is enough to justify their existence, but not big enough to deserve investment.

Spin-offs and new brands can work, but only after you have fully exploited the potential of your core brand and done everything possible to ensure it remains relevant and trusted in a changed world.

5   Don't be proud: pinch ideas from your disruptors

Earlier in this book, I warned against using either the likes of Google or Amazon – or smart little start-ups – as your role model. I stand by this; the underlying nature of your businesses is very, very different. The challenges you face in transforming a business are very different to those who have only known spectacular growth.

However, just because you're not fundamentally like them, doesn't mean you should ignore what they do and how they do it. When a new business tackles one of your core business problems in a way that you hadn't thought of, or didn't think was possible, your first instinct should be to find out more and ask whether and how this might be relevant to you. This is not the time to reject ideas simply because they weren't invented here.

Incumbents should see these start-ups as free R&D. If they manage to tap into a consumer need or want more effectively than you, you need to move quickly to emulate, appropriate, or to be blunt, simply copy (within the realms of the law) what they're doing. And speed is important, because whatever it is, it will take you much longer to deliver – and every day you delay allows new entrants to build momentum.

HMV, as we saw, should have quickly adopted Play.com's method of fulfilling internet orders from Jersey – and being able to offer much lower prices as a result. Newspapers have spent much time dismissing new content businesses such as the Huffington Post and Demand Media, for example. Energy spent on rubbishing these businesses is much better spent looking at how their processes and models could be reappropriated to their own needs.

6 Bring people with you

Embedded in this compact little phrase is the very essence of leadership: the ability to bring people with you through challenging times. And if ever there is a need for it – it is in a business going through profound structural change.

The 'people' that any leader is going to have to bring with them during this time will represent a broad church of internal and external stakeholders: staff, board members, customers, shareholders. There is no point developing the greatest transformation plan in living history if these vital constituencies are unconvinced: it is as close to a guarantee of failure as you can get.

The challenge is to present what you want, in their terms. It goes without saying then that being able to do this means first you have to have a pretty good idea of exactly what it is you want; and second you need to be aware of the sensitivities and concerns of each constituency. It means thinking and listening, not just talking: genuine communication, in other words.

Exactly how this is done depends on the style of the leader and the culture of the company. But what matters is that every piece of communication – internal and external, formal and informal – counts.

What also matters, is that decisions are not only made, but seen to be made – and explained. Debate and discussion are all healthy. The more people are engaged with the problems the business faces, the better. But at the end of the day, there needs to be complete clarity about the direction the business is heading in, and why.

This is especially true when there is bad news. Indeed, in every example of 'success' we have looked at, significant numbers of people have had to leave the companies concerned. This is traumatic for them; and often for those who stay who have to see friends and colleagues walking out the door against their will. If the process leaves people feeling that the executive team is either brutal or rudderless or some combination of the two then you will lose your very best people the second they can find something new to do.

In the box below I have highlighted the three Cs of bringing people with you – clarity, consistency and collaboration. There is a fourth that is equally important: common sense.

The three Cs of bringing people with you

Clarity

People need to know what is happening; why; how and when. If there is bad news, it needs to be explained clearly. If there is uncertainty, it is better to be open about it rather than trying to hide behind management speak and jargon. If there is a new strategy, it needs to be explained in a way that everyone in the business can understand. If there is a new structure, it needs to be clear who has responsibility for what. In times of complexity, there is a premium on simplicity. Fudging and fuzziness are the enemy.

Consistency

What you say and what you do needs to be consistent from one week to the next. If it isn't you need to have a very good

▶

▶

explanation, or you are providing a ready-made set of chinks in your armour for those who disagree with you. Don't just present a plan once; present it again and show how you have performed against it. If the plan evolves and changes, say why. You are leading people on a journey, not a set of random dance moves.

Collaboration

This is a time to get people working together. It is a time to see beyond silos. Getting people working with people from different parts of the business, tackling business problems collectively, is energising and constructive. It makes people feel they are part of something bigger than just their particular role. Create opportunities for collaboration – and, importantly, ensure that the results become reality. You will have stronger and more committed teams as a result.

7 Structure your business to reflect what's core and what's edge

The internet has caused a host of problems around organisational design – especially in businesses that previously produced a single product or distributed through a single channel. This has been particularly true in my own world, newspapers, where there has been a constant debate about whether the online business is a separate business unit or a set of functions – journalists, sales teams, marketing – that sit with their respective peers in the print business. The most dangerous assumption is that there is a 'right solution'. In fact the solution changes, reflecting the fundamental change in your business and the changing nature of what is 'edge' and what is 'core'.

ɢɢ the most dangerous assumption is that there is a 'right solution' ɢɢ

When we started the *Guardian*'s websites we sat in a different building: a completely separate business unit with its own profit and loss. It allowed us just the right mix of freedom and accountability. Over time, two things became clear. The digital team needed to be plugged into the main business in order to really reap the benefits of being part of the *Guardian*, rather than just being a start-up carrying the Guardian name. At the same time, the main newsroom needed to be able to use the internet as a means of telling their stories in the best possible way; and the sales teams increasingly needed to talk about the internet as part of their day-to-day offering. Integration was the way forward – and happened right through the business.

A similar thing happened in the UK arm of the WPP media agency, Mediacom, that was restructured in 2008. It went from being focused on individual media (print, TV, radio) – with 'digital' being its own unit – to being structured around individual types of media activity, each with 'digital' as an integral part: investment (buying media space to place advertising creative on); direct (search, direct response and e-commerce); and content (advertiser funded programming, gaming, mobile applications). This reflected the changing nature of the media buying business as a whole, not just the growth of 'digital'.

This process of integration is always tricky. The leap from simply rebadging your business ('news' not 'newspapers'), to genuinely redefining it is a massive one. The challenge isn't just about changing reporting lines and seating plans, but also changing processes and mindsets – and all of the techniques above need to be brought into play to make it work. Even when the core is integrated, though, there is still a need for edge activity, as we will see in the following chapters: nurturing the products and processes that will become part of the core; or developing the next big adjacency.

There is a next wave to this process and you can see it at Auto Trader in the UK. As I mentioned in Chapter 4, when Auto Trader's digital business started it sat on the edge of the business – competing, often aggressively with its print sibling. After nearly a decade of this, print and digital were brought together, effectively creating a united 'core' business.

After a couple of years, though, it became clear that the two businesses needed focus: the digital business in order to grow and see off an ever-growing number of competitors; the print business in order to generate as much cash as possible through a period of inevitable decline. At this point the 'core' business (and the largest profit generator) became digital, and the print business moved to the edge. Both benefited as a result.

I can see this happening with many classified businesses that started in print, as their markets move to being predominantly online their print businesses need a tighter focus. Newspaper editorial teams too might one day benefit from being detached from the minute-by-minute frenzy of their digital siblings. But not for sometime yet.

I want to close this chapter with two case histories – Deutsche Post and Nokia – which demonstrate, in their very different ways, the import-ance of fixing the core business before you go in pursuit of pastures new.

Deutsche Post and Nokia – how a strong core helps

In the next chapter we will look at the need for businesses to find big adjacencies if they want to grow through disruptive times. As we will see, there are plenty of pitfalls along the way in that process; but the greatest pitfall of all is to try and do it from a weakened core business.

The German postal service, Deutsche Post, and the world's largest handset manufacturer, Nokia, provide the perfect examples of attempts to find big adjacencies from core businesses in very different states of health.

Deutsche Post – expansion and innovation from a transformed core

In 1990, the German postal service, Deutsche Post, was state-owned and making a loss. In 2010, it sits at the core of the world's largest logistics business, now called Deutsche Post DHL. It is publicly owned, and profitable, despite the fact that its mail business, like those all over the world, is in terminal decline.

The key turning point for Deutsche Post happened way back in 1990 when it started a a ten-year transformation programme titled Letter 2000. This was sparked by the looming threat of privatisation, increased competition and the fact that after the Berlin Wall came down, they now had to extend their services to East Germany. At the time, they had no idea of the threat of the internet.

It was a massive programme. The number of mail centres was cut from 328 to 82, and the number of delivery centres reduced from 11,000 to 3,700. Advanced technology was installed throughout the network. It achieved this working with a union that represented 80% of the workforce. The financial result was that Deutsche Post went from a net loss of €720m in 1990 to breakeven point in the mid-1990s and from there into annually increasing profitability.

With this programme tackled Deutsche Post was to expand – into freight and logistics – a stream of acquisitions that have shifted the business away from dependency on a dying revenue stream – not all of these, as we will see in the next chapter, were successful. But, by 2009, 70% of their revenues came from outside the traditional mail business.

At the same time, not only have they expanded into freight and logistics, they have continued with the process of innovation and efficiency driving in their core mail business.

As CEO, Frank Appel said after his 2009 results came out:

The mail business is definitely going through an evolution. But we are prepared for it. Today, we are much more flexible than we were just a few years ago and we are able to react faster to shifting mail volumes... But we have to do even more in the future. We need to lower costs on a long-term basis. This is the only way to bolster profitability and secure jobs in the long run.[7]

The growth in e-commerce means greater volumes in parcels – and to meet this Deutsche Post have invested in the 'Packet Station' – a

---

7 Speaking on stage at DLD 2010, Hamburg, February 2010.

> **❝ this is the sweet spot of innovation ❞**

network of automated drop-off boxes where people can send and receive parcels. This is the sweet spot of innovation. Consumers love it, because it fits in with their wants and needs; Deutsche Post loves it because it saves them the 'last mile' cost of delivering parcels, to the door, and having to store them when people aren't in. And they are driving through digital innovation. In the summer of 2010, they launched a 'Letter on the Internet' that will allow secure digital transmission of items such as bills, invoices and financial statements – 'a milestone in digital written communication', according to Appel.

The decline of the postal service is a real and present threat to Deutsche Post. Nothing they have done, and nothing they could have done, will stem the decline. And they make no claims of false certainty about their future. Asked about the long-term health of the business, Appel says: 'Is there a tipping point when it's not profitable to have 80,000 postmen running round? I can't answer this – because we don't know how much our margins will drop.'[8]

When I spoke to their managing director of Corporate Development, Markus Reckling, he said one of the smartest things of anyone I spoke to while researching this book: 'I used to think that strategy was about avoiding unforeseen events; now I think it's about making sure you can deal with them.'[9] In other words, you cannot eliminate uncertainty – but if you want to be able to deal with it, it helps if you have the strongest possible core business to build from.

Nokia – the pursuit of adjacencies at the expense of the core

Nokia is one of the great success stories of the late 20th century. Emerging from a Finnish conglomerate that made everything from televisions to wellington boots, came a global business that dominated

---

8 Ibid.
9 In conversation with the author.

the mobile phone market for the best part of a decade, and saw sales rocket by tens of billions of dollars as a result.

But, in the late 1990s Nokia found itself losing ground to the likes of LG and Samsung. They picked up on a trend for clamshell phones that Nokia missed out on, and they also started to take share at the lower end of the market. Then came the Blackberry – which started to take share in the business market, and just to make matters worse, along came the iPhone.

Nokia's reaction to this was a strategic shift from being a handset manufacturer to software and services. They spent more than $10bn buying more than a dozen businesses to help them do this – the largest of which was Navteq, the mapping business bought for $8bn. Then they announced a massive reorganisation splitting itself into three divisions: handsets, software and services, and markets.

I spoke to quite a few Nokia executives during this period – and they all repeated the same mantra: 'the handset market has become commoditised; the future is in services'. It all made sense, apart from one thing – everyone in the world was getting phenomenally excited about new handsets and devices. We couldn't get enough of the latest gadgets from Apple, Blackberry and HTC – and Nokia handsets were becoming less appealling. Its Symbian operating system felt tired compared to Apple's iOS and Google's Android.

Nokia's market share fell from the magical 40% that they had once enjoyed. Not only that, they were losing share most rapidly at the top (i.e. the most profitable bit) of the market.

The problem was that the core of the business was creating handsets that people just had to have, and loved to use. That was what made Nokia great, and now other people were doing that better. According to an analyst at Deutsche Bank, Nokia's share of profit in the market dropped from 67% in 2007 to 32% in 2009.

Nokia's offerings seemed scattergun at best. Over 12 months they launched 20 high-end models: one every 18 days. It just looked like they were throwing cellphone spaghetti at the wall to see what might stick. *The Economist* reported on one analyst's view of their handsets:

Nokia has seemed to neglect its main business. The first version of its flagship smart-phone ... was a letdown. 'It has as many bells and whistles as a Swiss army knife,' says Caroline Milanesi of Gartner 'but its software ... makes them almost impossible to use ... it's like having a Ferrari body with a Fiat Cinquecento engine inside'.[10]

Nokia acted to fix the situation. They changed the management of their handsets division, and announced that they were going to focus on delivering fewer, better smartphones. There would be just ten in 2010 – with greater differentiation. But at the time of writing they are still losing ground to Apple, Android and Blackberry.

Strictly speaking, Nokia did not experience disruption. There was no sudden drop in barriers to entry. It was not a shift from analogue to digital. But there was a wave of radical innovation in the market – and the incumbent was left looking decidedly flat footed. Their insight – that the future value is in software and services was correct – but it meant they took their eye off the ball and they have been playing catch-up ever since.

10 'Nokia tries to re-invent itself: Bears at the door', *The Economist*, 7 January 2010.

6

Find big adjacencies

The process of 'core transformation' is critical, but it is not enough if your ambition is long-term, profitable growth. Even if you tick all of the boxes in the previous section, the net impact of the 'move to digital', combined with the other forces of creative disruption all too often results in businesses getting smaller. There are exceptions – such as Auto Trader – but they are few and far between.

There is a need for a bit of brutal honesty about the prospects for your business here. If you have seen 15% or more of your top line go, a mass of new competitors come into your market, and you are now having to manage both physical and digital businesses, then it simply isn't enough to hope that growth will come back to you, you have to go out and find it. For many businesses that have grown up offering a single product in a single market, that means a significant step out of your comfort zone. It means you have to look beyond your core business, and start to move into big adjacent markets: new geographies, or sectors, where your capabilities, customer relations or strategic insights give you some level of competitive advantage; and where there is a greater prospect for underlying growth, or at the very least greater resilience from disruption.

This is not about small experiments or minority stakes in interesting little businesses (we will discuss the role of these edge innovations later); the aim is to make a meaningful difference to the constitution of the company's revenues in a relatively short (less than five-year) period. In other words, it is either going to mean a few, very large, acquisitions or a lot of small to medium sized ones. As a result, this potentially carries both the highest risk, and the greatest reward of all of the strategies, tactics and suggestions in this book.

Here be monsters

There are two fundamental arguments against the pursuit of adjacencies through acquisition. First, is the academic argument that acquisitions in general tend to reduce shareholder value.

In *Why Acquisitions Fail*[1] Denzil Rankine gives a summary of research into the failure rate of acquisitions, and depending on the precise definition of 'failure' the rate lay between 50% and 80%. With any kind of move away from the core business, investor sentiment is even more negative. Shareholders will argue that if they want to put money into a different type of business, they will be better doing it themselves rather than entrusting it to an executive team that has no experience of that sector.

Secondly, there is a litany of disaster stories of traditional businesses buying their way into the digital world, any one of which can act as the perfect cold shower for any business warming to the idea of a big, digital acquisition. Mattel, for example, bought the educational software business, The Learning Company, at the height of the dotcom boom for $3.5bn (4× sales). In the year of the acquisition (1999), The Learning Company lost $200m on sales of $750m. The next year, the business was losing about $1.5m a day; and after only 18 months the business was sold – not for the $750m they had originally hoped, but given away in exchange for a share of future profits. But not before Mattel's shareholders had seen the value of

---

1 Denzil Rankine (2001), *Why Acquisitions Fail*, FT Prentice Hall (summary of research table available at www.pearsoned.co.uk/Bookshop/article.asp?item=439).

their stock halved, and Mattel's CEO Jill Barad had lost her job as a result.

Rupert Murdoch's acquisition of MySpace hasn't been as financially dramatic – but nor has it been the great success he might have hoped. After the initial benefits of seeing the News Corp share price rise as a result of the acquisition – and signing a $900m advertising deal with Google that promised to cover the acquisition price in one fell swoop – the business found itself falling behind to Facebook.

The revenues started to slip, and the slowdown in traffic meant that they didn't earn the money they had hoped from the Google deal. The investment was marked down on the balance sheet. A new chief executive was brought in to turn round the business, and then replaced within a year. The business went from being Murdoch's digital masterstroke, to a problem child within three years.

At around the same time as Murdoch bought MySpace, the UK's leading commercial broadcaster, ITV, paid £175m for Friends Reunited, the school reunion site that had grown like mad and charged people a small subscription fee for contacting their former classmates. At the time, it seemed like an unlikely acquisition and an astonishing price – and it proved to be so. Like MySpace, the business was undone by the growth of Facebook – and the fact that, frankly, once you had signed up and found out that you were neither the highest nor lowest achiever from your year, and exchanged a few stuttering e-mails, there wasn't really that much left to do. Even dropping the subscription fee didn't help matters.

❝ it seemed like an unlikely acquisition and an astonishing price ❞

Friends Reunited was sold three years later for £25m. The fact that it achieved even that valuation was the result of a move into the genealogy market, and the development of a small but profitable strand called Genes Reunited.

This combination of data and anecdotes should be enough to put anyone off buying a business ever again. But it does no such thing. Partly because not only is it human vanity to believe that even if 80% of acquisitions fail, you have what it takes to be one of the 20% that succeed; but also because acquisition is the fastest way to change the scale and shape of your organisation. Furthermore, acquisitions into adjacencies, I believe, provides the best strategic route to long-term growth and resilience.

We will look later at the danger of BDAs (big digital acquisitions) – and some of the lessons learned. We will also see that for some organisations a much more successful strategy is to move into things that simply can't be digitised – what I describe as a retreat to the physical. Finally we'll see how five different newspaper groups have fared with very different approaches to seeking big adjacencies.

But first, I want to look at two businesses in very different sectors that have managed to avoid disruption and decline through decades of successful acquisitions and a constant pursuit of the next adjacency: WPP and Cisco.

Cisco Systems and WPP – the long-term success of continuously evolving corporations

Cisco operates in the world of networked technology; WPP is one of the world's leading marketing services organisations. In terms of what they do, they are miles apart. But in terms of how they operate – and how they have managed to sustain a formidable position within their markets for the past two decades – they have three very important things in common.

1   Consistency in leadership

Sir Martin Sorrell founded WPP in 1985 and has been at the helm ever since. John Chambers joined Cisco in 1991 and became CEO in 1995. The shape of both businesses has been driven by the men at the top.

In an era when CEOs are deemed to have done a fair innings if they serve for five years, these two tenures are quite exceptional.

This consistency in leadership becomes twinned with a consistency in strategic direction: WPP and Cisco sit in fast-moving markets. The constituency of the groups has changed dramatically over the years – but having the same man at the top has been a critical part of their success. It is part of what I believe is a critical factor as a company moves away from its core: a strong internal sense of the corporate DNA.

2   Sustained growth through acquisition into adjacent markets

Cisco and WPP have, between them, made some 200 acquisitions in their histories, and the sustaining theme has been the continuous movement into adjacent markets to meet the changing needs of their customers, and to tap into growth markets.

WPP has expanded from being a business primarily focused on advertising in the UK and USA, into a global marketing services business. Cisco has moved from its origins as a router business to positions right across the world of networked technologies.

The following is John Chambers' explanation to the *Harvard Business Review* of how some of his earlier acquisitions were driven by satisfying customer demand:

Sometimes, the customer can be pretty blunt. I met once with one who said, 'John, here's a $10 million order you're not going to get unless you buy this [other] company.' I left that meeting with a $10 million check in my pocket and a commitment in my mind to acquire Crescendo, which we did. We paid $92 million for a company with less than $10 million in revenue in 1993, and a lot of analysts thought we were crazy. But that turned into a $7 billion a year business for our switching unit. The same kind of thing happened when we acquired Scientific Atlanta in 2006. Our internet service provider (ISP) customers told us they needed network support for video, so it made sense to buy one of the only companies that had mastered the art and science of delivering video.[2]

2 Bronwyn Fryer and Thomas A. Stewart (2008) 'Cisco Sees The Future', *Harvard Business Review*, November.

Sorrell talks consistently about three priority areas for his business: the BRIC and 'next 11' economies; the internet; and the growth of customer insight. As a result he continues to both drive change within his existing businesses, and make acquisitions to make sure that each of these three areas account for 30% of his business. This has meant a mix of transformational change within his existing businesses, but also the $1bn acquisition of Taylor Nelson Sofres in 1998 to bolster his consumer insight division, and the $690m acquisition of the digital advertising technology business, 24/7 RealMedia.

Even when WPP isn't making full blown acquisitions, it has a very active wave of investments in digital start-ups – as we will see in Chapter 7 when we look at corporate venturing.

Cisco similarly shows no sign of curtailing its ambitions. The company has made a string of big acquisitions into the world of collaboration tools, buying WebEx for $2.7bn in 2007, and the video conferencing specialist Tanberg for $3.4bn.

Cisco's annual report for 2009 states that the business is 'addressing no fewer than 30 market adjacencies, mostly in areas where networking technologies and protocols have not seen widespread adoption. Industries such as healthcare, sport, entertainment and utilities, as well as emerging geographic markets provide significant opportunities to provide growth for Cisco and value to customers and shareholders'.

Not every acquisition that these two companies made has worked out brilliantly – what matters though is that this is an entrenched process, and part of their overall growth strategy. Both organisations have well-defined processes for defining targets, carrying out due diligence, securing approval and managing the vital period after acquisition. As with most things, the more you do it – the better you get.

3   The near-death moment

This has not been achieved without its difficulties. Both businesses have had to recover from over-stretching themselves.

In 1992, after two huge acquisitions of J Walter Thompson and the Ogilvy Group (for which Sorrell paid 42 × earnings) WPP was saddled with around $1bn in debt. When the recession hit, the company teetered on the brink of bankruptcy – an ongoing saga. At one stage the finance director was having to approve the weekly payroll.[3] Eventually, a debt-for-equity deal was struck with the banks, and WPP.

In Chambers case, at one stage during the dotcom boom Cisco had the largest market capitalisation of any company on earth – but it all came crashing down as their sales went into decline after the dotcom crash. Between March 2000 and March 2001, their share price – which had only previously known growth – dropped from $77 to $16 as a result.

While Sorrell's problem stemmed from a small number of very large acquisitions, at Cisco, part of the problem was they started to buy too many companies too early. In order to keep ahead of the competition, Cisco went from buying companies that were pre-profit, to pre-revenue **66** a waste of cash and effort all round **55** and pre-product. An article in *Business Week*[4] gave the example of Monterey Networks acquired at the peak of Cisco's buying spree in August 1999 for half a billion dollars. It was one of four companies bought that month, and it had no revenue, and no products. At the time of purchase it had simply run up hundreds of millions of dollars of losses since its launch. Some 18 months after the acquisition, Cisco shut it down. A waste of cash and effort all round.

But, both businesses – and chief executives – survived. Chastened, but also more resilient.

4   Surviving the downturn

The lessons from these two near-death moments is that both businesses survived the recession of 2008 and 2009 in relatively good shape. Both

3 www.forbes.com/forbes/2008/0421/128.html
4 John A. Byrne and Ben Eigin (2002) 'Cisco Shopped till it Nearly Dropped', *Business Week*, 21 January.

organisations carry the risk of sitting in areas where businesses will cut first: major capital expenditure programmes for Cisco, and advertising spend for WPP.

Both were challenged; and both saw falls in their top lines. Both had to cut costs as a result, but thanks to the diversifications of the previous decade, both were also much more robust businesses than they had been a decade or so earlier. The table below shows just how much both businesses had grown between the boom of 1999 and the downturn of 2009.

Revenues	1999	2009
WPP	£2.1bn	£8.6bn
Cisco Systems	$12.15bn	$36.1bn

Their success is obviously not just about acquisitions; and it does both Sorrell and Chambers a disservice to think that all they have done is buy growth. As well as the transformation efforts happening at divisional level within WPP, Sorrell delivered an industry first when he created a dedicated agency by pulling together all the necessary ingredients from his group in order to win Dell's $4.5bn global account.

But without the wave of continuous acquisition, these businesses would not have achieved the scale and resilience that saw them through the recession.

The two critical elements of successful adjacency strategies

Chris Zook's *Beyond the core*,[5] is in my mind the definitive textbook on expansion into adjacencies. Zook and his team from Bain Consulting analyse the data from hundreds of companies that have tried to expand into adjacencies – and I cannot recommend it highly enough.

---

5 Chris Zook (2004) *Beyond the Core*, Harvard Business School Press.

He comes up with two key conclusions, both of which fit with what we have just seen from WPP and Cisco.

Go far enough, but not too far

First, the most successful businesses at finding adjacencies normally go no more than two or three 'steps' away from their core business. The idea of a 'step' is loosely defined, based on customers, competitors, cost structure, capabilities and distribution channels. If you fail to move a few steps away from your core business, then you aren't really breaking into an adjacency. If you go too far – as happened with Mattel and The Learning Company mentioned above – it is likely that you simply won't know enough about the sector you are moving into to be able to add any value to the acquisitions.

Practice makes perfect

The second key lesson is about 'repeatability' – in other words, the best businesses work out the process for doing this over and over again. This includes the following:

■ selection criteria for a target (which saves time filtering the countless opportunities that get thrown in your direction by investment bankers once they know you are in acquisition and expansion mode)
■ what to focus on, and dig deep into, during due diligence
■ what process to go through to secure board approval
■ what to do once the business has been acquired.

We'll see both of these conclusions appear again when we look at how the two newspaper groups, Schibsted and Naspers, have approached their adjacency strategies.

These are good generic examples, but the era of creative disruption also delivered two very specific areas for adjacencies that deserve attention on their own – the danger of the BDA (big digital acquisition) and the value of a retreat to the physical.

The danger of the BDA

The examples I gave in the section above highlight the danger of the big digital acquisition (BDA). It happens when a big organisation feels it has fallen somewhat behind in the digital world, and therefore it needs to do something big, fast. MySpace, The Learning Channel and Friends Reunited were all examples of this.

The greatest mistake that any traditional business buying a digital business can make is to look at the size of its audience and assume that because they know how they would make money from a business of that size in the physical world, they have the capabilities to instantly turn this massive, but loss-making entity into a business with sustainable profits.

This buyer's conceit is something that those who package up and sell businesses for a living know all too well how to play on. Venture capitalists, for example, know that if they can create a strong growth business with a large active audience, it is sometimes better to leave it with the potential for generating significant revenues and profits rather than actually going through the process of trying to deliver it yourself.

" converting that audience into money is a delicate skill "

The problem is that buying a website with 10 million users is not the same as buying a magazine with 10 million subscribers, or a shop with 10 million people passing through its aisles but not buying enough. Converting that audience into money is a delicate skill, and one that very few traditional businesses have proved themselves adept at. And there are two big challenges: first, you have to keep investing to keep, let alone grow, your audience; second, the money might simply not be there.

Once a business is acquired, the focus then often shifts onto trying to deliver the financial results that justify the acquisition price, rather than continuing to invest in a product that will delight users. And given that users can desert most digital services with the click of a mouse, it is very, very easy to lose your audience to whoever has taken all the lessons you have learned, and simply rolled out a better service.

In addition, the lack of profitability in the business, or revenues that might seem small given the overall scale of the audience, is often an intrinsic part of the operation, not simply a sign that the management team don't know how to make money. Two of the internet's biggest sites, Craigslist and Wikipedia, have very small revenues compared to their enormous audiences – but changing the way these sites are commercialised – either by adding advertising to them or looking at charging people for various elements – would upset the delicate ecosystem that makes these sites so attractive to users.

Does this mean that no-one should buy digital businesses? Far from it. But it is a particularly prickly process. I offer three tips based both on experience and observation.

1   Get your processes right and repeat them

This goes back to one of the points mentioned above. I spoke to one publisher who had bought a digital content site with a massive audience but very small revenues. 'It took us 18 months longer than we thought to get the revenue to a decent level,' he told me. The problem was that delay had been seen by their board as a sign of failure, and the reason they shouldn't make another acquisition. In truth, the best way to extract value from the lessons learned in this first acquisition was to follow it up with a second and then a third.

2   Look for marketplaces

It is incredibly easy to lose a digital audience – but one of the key insurances against this is to find targets where buyers and sellers convene – and where both sides have to use the service if they want to be in the market. In the UK, Auto Trader and Rightmove are two such examples. Both have been deluged with competition – but in both cases they have seen it off, and managed to continue to put their prices up. If you are looking to either buy or sell a car or house in the UK, it's a very, very brave move not to use them. This makes these businesses much more defensible than others with similar audience numbers. Any competitor has to lure away both buyers and sellers if they want to make a real impact – and the cost of that is almost always shockingly prohibitive.

3   Buy the sausage, not the sizzle

It is better by far to focus on what the business is, rather than what it could be. As I have said, buyer's conceit is a dangerous factor in any acquisition, especially in digital ones where the potential for growth is always a dizzying set of geographic and market expansions. For all the reasons mentioned above, a large audience that isn't delivering meaningful revenues is something to be deeply cautious of – not something to get excited about. Due diligence is no-one's idea of fun, but it is critical in working out exactly what it is you are buying, and checking that there is something truly distinctive and defensible there. Oh, and a simple rule of thumb – factor in the cost of rebuilding the technology. For some reason, that nearly always has to happen.

The retreat to the physical

We have seen from the outset how digitisation challenges incumbent businesses – no matter what area they operate in – but especially in content businesses and in sectors such as the mail. The growth of the digital world has created a potential for investment in digital adjacencies – but it has also placed an increasing premium on products and services that simply can't be digitised. This is why we have seen Deutsche Post move from letters – that are constantly being substituted by e-mail and other digital services – into the world of freight and logistics, where digital technology can make the businesses more efficient, but there is no threat of substitution. TNT in the Netherlands has followed exactly the same route.

We will also see, when we look at Kodak, that their most profitable business is in the professional film market – especially around movies, where the world of chemicals and celluloid still has a role to play. It is also why we have seen continued growth in the live music market – and the strength of Livenation and Ticketmaster as a result, while record labels have struggled in the face of declining revenues from recorded music. Smart music organisations – whether large or small – will be buying up businesses that have a foothold in the growth markets of Asia and China, as well as a strong position in the live music value chain.

Figure 6.1 shows the shift in how United Business Media has evolved its operating profits over five years. The decline in print magazines has been somewhat covered by the growth in online and data services, but the real growth for them has come in the one bit of their business that can't be digitised – events (conferences and exhibitions). In a world of ubiquitous e-mail and corporate websites, there is still a premium on face-to-face meetings and, as a result, owning the key event in any industry's calendar – the exhibition that people feel they just have to be at – has become more important rather than less.

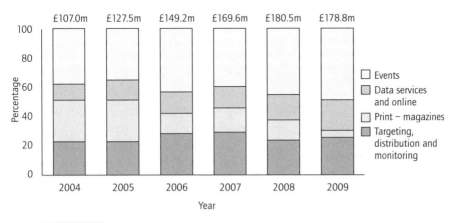

Figure 6.1 United Business Media's retreat to the physical

Source: http://www.ubm.com/ubm/ir/presentations/2010/2010-03-05a/2010-03-05a.pdf, page 3, reproduced with permission.

UBM is busy experimenting with a number of 'virtual exhibition' formats that allow once annual events to take on a digital presence throughout the year – but for the moment at least, this is a much more complementary activity than a substitutional one.

One of the great ironies of the digital world is that everyone relishes any opportunity for a physical gathering as a result of it – whether that be a big conference such as Web 2.0, SXSW or TED, or simply a gathering of people who happen to use Twitter and live or work in the same area – 'A tweet up'. Even the most wired people in the world love being in the same room as each other. The businesses that enable that are sitting on something very powerful indeed.

In summary, often the most straightforward way to reduce your exposure to the disruption of the digital world is to invest away from it.

Take five: newspaper groups in search of adjacencies

Newspaper companies provide us with a rich set of examples in this area. This is partly because they demonstrate the need for disrupted businesses to move into adjacencies to deliver growth, but also because we can see a set of different strategies for seeking adjacencies – and a different set of consequent results.

Newspaper groups have plenty of options when seeking an adjacent market: they can either choose to consolidate in the press market; or move into any one of a number of adjacencies expanding within their geographic market, within the news media, into a vertical where they have strength, or the broader media market. And, over the past few decades, pretty much every possible avenue has been taken by one group or another.

We are going to look at five different businesses to see how they compare and contrast. First the UK's Johnston Press – a domestic consolidator. Next we'll look at the difference between the New York Times Company and the Washington Post – thanks to the latter's decision to move into the education market in the late 1980s. Finally we'll look at the Norwegian Schibsted and South African Naspers: the two businesses most analysts believe had done the best job of surviving the onslaught of the internet, and which have been most aggressive in pursuit of digital adjacencies.

Why do it in the first place?

Perhaps the single most important point to make right up front is that the organic initiatives that have taken place within all of these newspapers – especially their ventures online – are important, and in some cases truly impressive, but in terms of overall corporate health they are marginal. In 2009, the US newspaper industry had a terrible year in print – but also saw its digital revenues fall by 11%. When you consider that those revenues are, in most cases, less than 15% of total company revenues, it is clear that even the most successful players have yet to find the path through to organic growth by developing their own websites and managing the cost base in their print business.

The figures from Norwegian publisher Schibsted (see Table 6.1) shows us the limits of what can be achieved even when you get things absolutely right.

Table 6.1   Schibsted data, 2005–09 (millions of Norwegian kroner)

	2005	2006	2007	2008	2009	CAGR*
Verdens Gang	248	209	241	214	255	0.56%
Verdens Gang Multimedia	51	82	119	109	69	6.23%
VG total	**299**	**291**	**360**	**323**	**324**	1.62%
Aftonbladet	207	222	211	192	106	−12.53%
Aftonbladet Nya Medier	30	76	60	87	57	13.70%
Aftonbladet total	**237**	**298**	**271**	**279**	**163**	−7.21%

*Compound Annual Growth Rate

Table 6.1 shows the EBIT of Schibsted's two most successful newspapers, Norway's *Verdens Gang* (normally known as VG) and Sweden's *Aftonbladet*. They have both done a brilliant job of building profitable web businesses, and they both have the advantage of delivering services in languages (Norwegian and Swedish) where there is comparative scarcity online. They were also early investors in mobile and video, and have built up strong online advertising franchises on top of millions of users. Finally, they have introduced a number of successful paid for services: *Aftonbladet*'s diet club was a cause célèbre among newspaper businesses around the world.

And yet, even with all of this effort – and a very resilient performance in print from VG – the total profit from the two titles combined just about managed to stay flat between 2005 and 2008, and then fell in 2009.

Schibsted's performance here is still exceptional when benchmarked against their peers. But even so, for real growth – as we shall see – they have had to look elsewhere.

The cautionary tale of Johnston Press

The UK regional newspaper publisher, Johnston Press, is the classic, single country, single medium player. In the good times, they looked

Mar 24, 2000 – Mar 23, 2010

——— FTSE 100 –13.72%   ——— JPR –90.68%

Figure 6.2 From hero to near zero – Johnston Press's performance against the FTSE 100 index over a decade

Source: Google Finance, reproduced with permission.

very good; but in bad times, they looked very, very bad (see Figure 6.2). Johnston Press was the darling of the City in the early 2000s.

In the aftermath of the dotcom collapse, when it looked as though newspapers were a much more resilient business than many digital zealots might have claimed, banks happily threw money at them to let them buy up dozens of titles around the country. Johnston Press picked up a host of major assets including the *Scotsman*, the Scottish national daily, that they acquired in 2005 for £160m. As they acquired, they drove out efficiencies and delivered market-leading 30% margins.

" at one stage the share price was around 5 pence "

JP's share price soared. At their peak, their market capitalisation was around £1.2bn. When in 2004/05, the ad market started to slow down, JP initially seemed to be immune. However, this proved to be somewhat optimistic. When the downturn turned into a recession, revenues started to fall and everything came undone. Their valuation plummeted and rumours swirled about Johnston's debts. At one stage the share price was around 5 pence.

In 2008, there was a rights issue; then in the summer of 2009, with a new chief executive in place (Tim Bowdler the previous chief executive retired, admitting he had presided over a dramatic decline in shareholder value), the debt was renegotiated at a cost of a cool £15m (a significant price for a business of this size).

At the end of this roller coaster ride, what are we left with? By March 2010, JP's market cap was less than £180m – only marginally more than they paid for the *Scotsman*. Those stellar operating margins stood at 17%, down from around 30%, and they have had to take impairments on their publishing operation of some £500m. Only a small amount of their revenues come from the internet.

JP's consolidation strategy had impressed in the short term, but simply stored up trouble for the future. Acquisition and margin improvement help deliver great results in a stable or growing market, but in a sector facing structural change they were simply buying more of the same problems.

Two great American newspapers; two very different businesses.

The *New York Times* and *Washington Post* might well be peers in the newspaper world – but the companies that own them are very, very different. And their performance in the torrid year of 2009 (see Table 6.2), and their prospects for the coming decade, are very different as a result.

Table 6.2 2009 results for the New York Times Company and the Washington Post Company

2009 results	Total revenues ($m)	Year on year % ($m)	Operating profit+ ($m)	Core newspaper* revenues ($m)	Year on year %	Net income
New York Times Company	2,400	−24.5	74	1,581	−17.5	1.6
Washington Post Company	4,600	+2.0	193	679	−15	91.2

*For NYT, Core newspaper = New York Media Group; for Washington Post Company, core = 'newspaper group'

+After depreciation, amortisation and severance charges

The *New York Times* is one of the world's great newspapers. Both in print and online it is hugely respected creatively and commercially; and newspaper executives from around the world beat a path to its doors to get a glimpse of how it works. But the recession of 2008/09 proved that even a newspaper business with a great title at its helm is still a newspaper business – and vulnerable as a result.

The New York Times Company owns the *Times*, the *Boston Globe* – bought in 1991 for a staggering $1.1bn – and a host of smaller titles. These businesses with their accompanying websites and other content businesses account for 95% of the company's revenues. Their one significant non-print business is About.com bought for $410m in 2005. About.com is a star in the making, with 40%+ margins, and without its contribution in 2009, the business's bottom line would have looked particularly unhealthy.

As the recession hit, trading turned from bad to worse, the company cut their dividend, and announced lay-offs. But there was also $400m debt due in the spring of 2009, and they needed to refinance – no small feat in the middle of a credit crunch. And so, in February 2009, the company announced that they were taking a $250m investment from the world's richest man, Carlos Slim. Slim ended up with 17% of the business, and a new class of shares that gave him a quite spectacular 14% interest.

For all of the prestige of their core title, the combination of debt, a downturn and disruption left the New York Times Company as vulnerable as Johnston Press.

Two hundred miles down the road, the *Washington Post* had an even more shocking financial year in 2009, making an operating loss of some $163m – an effective loss of some $450,000 a day. It was a terrible year for the newspaper; but as you can see from Table 6.2, the company proved to be more resilient, for the simple reason that they are no longer a newspaper company. As their website, and every piece of corporate communications they offer reminds us, they are 'a diversified education and media company'.

The newspaper group at the Washington Post Company makes up less than 15% of total revenues. The bulk – 60% – comes from Kaplan, its education business; with another 15% coming from cable television, Cable One. In 2009, these businesses generated operating income of $194m and $164m respectively, wiping out the losses of the newspaper group.

This performance is the result of two comparatively small moves made some 20 years ago. Kaplan was acquired in 1984 for $33m;

Cable One started its life as Post-Newsweek Cable in 1986, with the acquisition of a service with 350,000 subscribers from Capital Cities/ABC. Both businesses have been built up over the years with subsequent acquisitions, the largest of which seems to have been Kaplan's $178m acquisition of the Quest Education Corporate in 2000. It is difficult to acquire all the numbers, but it's a pretty safe bet that the total cost of building up these businesses was less than the $1.1bn the New York Times paid for the *Boston Globe*.

This comparison isn't intended to flatter the *Post* or chastise the *Times* – Kaplan has been a much greater success than anyone might have imagined, and writing in *Vanity Fair*, media commentator Michael Wolff said they bought the company 'for no more prescient reason than that it was cheap'. But for whatever reason, the two businesses took the routes they took and have ended up in very different places as a result. As well as the headline lesson that diversified businesses are more resilient through structural change, they teach us two basic lessons as a result.

Lesson 1: Small move into a big adjacency is a good place to start

Education is a big market. So is Cable TV. The initial investments into both of these markets were relatively modest but provided a good platform for growth. It may well be that these initial acquisitions were simply tactical responses to opportunities that walked through the door rather than strokes of strategic genius, but what matters is what happened next. A small move into a big market, followed up with sustained investment, has the potential to be truly transformative.

Lesson 2: You still have to fix the core

❝ hundreds of jobs have already gone ❞

The *Washington Post* is the emotional heart of the business. For the Graham family, the largest shareholder in the business, this is much more than a financial asset. But even this connection, and the prosperity that comes from Kaplan, doesn't mean the business can continue to haemorrhage cash at the current rate. It faces competition on every front: from Craigslist taking their classifieds, to the political media specialists, Politico, launching a dedicated Washington news site. Hundreds of jobs have already gone in their news room. Sections have folded. I suspect there will be plenty more bad news before there is good.

Naspers and Schibsted: adjacency seekers on steroids

The *Washington Post's* moves into education and cable TV protected their business against the disruption of the digital world. But these moves were made well before the internet reared its head; with the current management reaping the rewards of their predecessors' decisions.

Our next two examples feature two businesses that aggressively charged at the internet as it appeared, not just reinventing their newspaper businesses, but breaking into the online world with quite dramatic success: Naspers from South Africa, and Schibsted from Norway.[6]

Schibsted's roots were in newspapers in Norway and Sweden. Over the years they expanded into broadcast ('Live Pictures' as it appears on their results); but when the internet emerged they expanded instantly and aggressively into the world of online only classifieds through a mix of acquisitions and organic launches, and rolling out successful models internationally. Blocket, for example, is their core classified business in Sweden – a place where people buy and sell pretty much everything, and a business with a 56% margin. They acquired this in 2003, and there are now versions of it in more than a dozen countries from Spain to the Philippines.

Schibsted's results between 2005 and 2009 (see Table 6.3) show the dramatic decline in the profitability of their newspapers; but also the fact that even if you add the EBITA of the newspapers and

---

6 I should declare here that Eniro, the Nordic's directory business on whose board I sit, is a direct competitor to Schibsted.

their websites together you end up with less than the EBITA of the newspapers alone in 2005.[7]

Table 6.3 Schibsted Group, EBITA 2005–09 (millions of Norwegian kroner)

	2005	2006	2007	2008	2009	CAGR
Print newspapers	695	690	759	460	409	−10.06%
Online newspapers	85	148	127	102	5	−43.26%
Classifieds/directories	104	140	398	561	641	43.87%
Live pictures	93	60	−40	−14	−12	−166.40%
Schibsted Group	955	993	1,157	766	832	−2.72%

Most of all though, it is clear that the growth of the separate, online only classified businesses have helped to maintain overall group profitability. Without their contribution, the group overall would be barely profitable.

Naspers was founded in 1915 as Die Nasionale Pers in Johannesburg. It was *the* Afrikaans media company – starting in newspapers and then moving into magazines and books. The leader columns of its daily newspaper, *Die Burger*, supported apartheid until the very end. But, if their newspaper's politics were rooted in the past, their business vision was firmly rooted in the future. In 1995, Naspers moved into pay TV, which is now their most profitable business. And then, when the internet appeared, they set up an ISP, M-Web.

Like Schibsted they were aggressive in attacking the opportunities of the internet right from the start – but they went one step further than the digital version of their core classified business. Their focus is on pure internet businesses in developing countries – especially those with an e-commerce or social dimension.

---

7 The overall performance of Schibsted's newspapers, both print and online, is pulled down by some of its poorer performing titles. Their main Norwegian tabloid *VG*, has managed to hold up remarkably well in print, and as a result total EBITA (print and online) rose between 2005 and 2009 by a CAGR of 1.62%. Their other key title, *Aftonbladet*, saw its online EBITA double over the period, but its print result halved, therefore combined EBITA fell by a CAGR of −7.2%.

The jewel in their crown is their 35% share in Tencent, the leading Chinese social network, that they acquired for around $30m in 2001. By the end of 2009 this was worth around $30bn as an asset. What makes this story even more impressive is that this was Naspers' second investment in China – the first went wrong, resulting in the loss of tens of millions of dollars. However, they went back, and struck gold.

But, beyond this Naspers have more than 100 internet investments in different developing markets. They own Russia's biggest e-mail service Mail.ru, the Polish online community Gadu Gadu, Eastern European auction site Ricardo, and a host of businesses from Vietnam to Brazil – in all they have businesses in 28 cities in 20 countries. The beauty of this more radical interpretation of their capabilities is that they have escaped the rather cyclical nature of classified advertising. Their results show that in 2009 the operating profit from their internet businesses outstripped their print business for the first time (see Figure 6.3).

Schibsted's and Naspers' areas of focus have been different – but they stand above the rest of the newspaper pack; and their strategies have five key things in common.

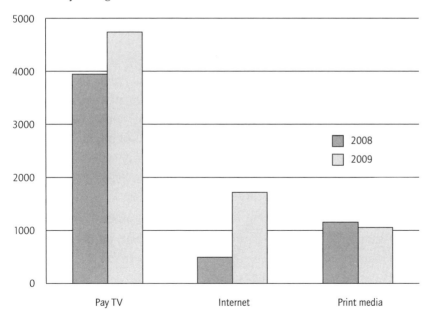

Figure 6.3   The rise of online: Naspers – operating profits 2008 and 2009

1 **They started early, and continued to invest and acquire their internet businesses after the dotcom crash.** Both businesses had chief executives who were committed to the internet right from the start – and they carried on investing throughout. This continuous restlenessness is still there in both businesses: at the time of writing, both are still actively looking for new areas to invest in.

2 **Their internet businesses have always been free to compete with their traditional businesses.** This was a particular issue for Schibsted, given that they were often operating in the same market as their newspapers. In fact, they used their newspapers' online presences to help build reach for their online classified businesses.

3 **They were both forced to think internationally immediately because of the limited potential in their domestic markets.** The ability to adapt a winning formula in a different geographic market provides a potent capability for expansion. For both Naspers and Schibsted, this was never an option. If they wanted their digital businesses to achieve true scale, they had to expand internationally. As a result, even after all of this activity neither business is anywhere near its maximum potential.

4 **They continuously repeat and refine their processes.** 'Repeatability', as defined by Chris Zook is a critical factor in both company's approaches. With each deal, they get better. Hein Pretorius, who runs Naspers Internet Investments programme outlines a set of criteria for any business they are looking at. For example, they always use local management, and look for entrepreneurs and founders who are committed to the business. If the business is run by a serial entrepreneur, they will leave it. As a result, they have managed to keep the founders in place at every one of their businesses.[8]

5 **The core still counts.** Just as with the Washington Post, all of this activity doesn't remove the obligation to focus on the core business. For Naspers this means continuing to drive for growth in its PayTV business, while Schibsted remains an excellent and efficient newspaper publisher.

---

8 Interviewed on stage at DLD 2010, Hamburg.

7

Innovate at the edges

The two main strategic objectives for any business facing disruption are to transform its core business and – if possible – to find big adjacencies. To make both of these happen, you need a continuous wave of innovation at the edge of your business. Transforming your core business means you need new products and processes if you are going to become a new business. This might be developed internally or bought in from outside. Similarly, the pursuit of a big adjacency often starts with a relatively small step – spinning out a small revenue stream that has potential for significant growth outside the core business, or making an investment or acquisition of an interesting start-up.

I put all of these activities under the banner of 'edge innovations', whose importance is far greater than their absolute size and as such need a disproportionate amount of focus and attention.

The first thing that is important, then, about edge innovations is that they are there to serve a strategic purpose – and not an end in their own right. Consequently, what you have to ask about any edge innovation, no matter how it is going to be delivered, is 'Why are we doing this?' If the answer isn't either 'because it will help us improve our core business' or 'because we believe it is going to open up a big new opportunity for us' then it is a non-starter. It might be an interesting or fascinating project, it might even make a bit of money, but if it doesn't fit one of these two criteria, then it simply isn't important enough for you to devote scarce resource to.

The next thing that is critical about edge innovations is that having too many of them at any one time is a massive diversion. As a result, being 'edge' innovation is rather like being in hospital: the priority is to get you out of there fit and well as soon as possible. Our edge innovation either goes into the core business or it becomes a fully fledged business unit on its own. If it's not going to make it then, unfortunately, it is kinder to pull the plug than spend years languishing in intensive care.

A lot of the scrutiny around innovation activity – especially when it's presented to boards – is about the last of these scenarios: 'What are you going to do when it fails?' That is a relatively easy problem – even though the solution is often painful. The challenge is what to do when it succeeds – and how to move it away from its temporary position as an edge innovation into something that has a real impact.

Ideas, you see, are cheap, but great execution is priceless. And great execution isn't just about the initial act of conception of a new product, service or process – it's not about the cool prototype or the demo, it's about about being able to make something happen within your organisation.

Scientists at Kodak created the first digital camera in 1975. It was a cumbersome beast, bearing no relation to the kind of digital cameras today. But they were there first. It was, however, a wasted innovation. Not because it was way ahead of its time and, in its first iteration, of not much obvious immediate commercial use, but because it posed a direct threat to the core business, and there was no way for it to prosper within Kodak.

> **❝ Kodak let Sony, Canon and Fuji steal a march on them ❞**

As a result, despite their lead in technical innovation, Kodak let Sony, Canon and Fuji steal a march on them in the world of digital photography, as they battled on, defending film for nearly another 30 years.

Because of this, you have to follow Rule number one – 'begin with the end in mind' – from Stephen Covey's famous book, *Seven*

Habits of Highly Effective People. If this is a product or process that is going to be integrated into the core business, someone needs to be thinking from the earliest possible moment about how to mitigate some of the inevitable pitfalls that come from this kind of integration. Who will need to be convinced that this is a good idea, and when should we speak to them? What customers should we be testing it out on? What skills are we likely to need to bring in? Who will need retraining?

If this is going to flourish into the next big adjacency, then there are really five big questions:

- Who is going to run it?
- Are we clear about what advantage we bring to this sector and how we're going to exploit it?
- What functions/resources will it share with the existing business?
- Are there any clashes/competition issues with the existing business, and how will we manage them?
- Will we have enough cash to fund the necessary expansion that will follow?

Build or buy – know your limits

The debate about whether you should do this yourself, or buy a company that is already in the market will rear its head within minutes of any serious discussion about innovation.

There is no right answer here. Table 7.1 overleaf outlines some of the positives and negatives for both buying and building depending on what you are trying to achieve with your innovation. But, here, generic truisms melt away in the face of the specific capabilities and experiences within an organisation.

For me, though, there is one plan that should always spark a flashing red light – and that is the proposal for a corporate to do its own start-up in the hope that you can tap into a big adjacent market. The first attempt at the numbers look good, but either it is too disruptive of the core business or it is something that simply won't get the attention it needs. Consequently, it is decided that the best thing to do is to make it a separate unit of its own – effectively a start-up within a corporate. For those who have always fancied themselves as entrepreneurs but felt held back by the corporate structure, the idea is just too good to resist.

Table 7.1 Pros and cons of building and buying

What are you trying to achieve?	Build +	Build −	Buy +	Buy −
Develop a product, process or service for core transformation	You can create something from scratch with integration in mind	Internal consensus can result in a less optimal solution	You bring in expertise as well as an up and running entity	Integration challenges are large. Difficult to get under the skin before you get hold of the keys
Find a big adjacency	Internal teams have access to all assets	Are you really the best people to start up a business? Can you make it big enough, quick enough?	You bring in expertise and scale instantly	Standard dangers of bad acquisition: poor selection, due diligence, and danger you overestimate the value you can add, and overpay as a result

The problems with this approach are many:

- A great executive in a corporate – normally the person who gets given responsibility for something like this – is not necessarily the best person to launch a business from scratch. Entrepreneurs and executives are very different people.

- The accountability required in the corporate world can often burden the initiative with both costs and reporting responsibilities that stifle a business in the early days.

■ Being a completely stand-alone unit makes the operation very vulnerable in a downturn. If it isn't making a meaningful contribution quickly, it will rapidly face the axe.

■ Even if it is successful (and as with all start-ups, the odds are that it won't be), it will take years to achieve scale.

This is not always the case, but it is something to be very wary off. And I speak from experience. During the dotcom boom, we carried out some strategy work at the *Guardian* around our recruitment business. It was clear that our print business was destined to decline, and that our internal efforts to build up a digital recruitment presence under the Guardian brand would only take us so far. Even though we dominated our specialist areas (media, education, public sector) we had no presence in the broader recruitment market.

So, we did a start-up. It was called Workthing – and sat separately to the main business, free to operate as it liked as long as it didn't compete with the *Guardian* in its core market. It didn't work. Workthing struggled as a business and relationships with the *Guardian* were strained. In the end it was sold on at a loss.

With hindsight, we should have realised we weren't the people to start a business from scratch: even with the help of a chief executive brought in from outside. We should have looked to acquire one of the more successful job boards that already existed: something with the scale and stature to compete directly with us, and also with a proven record of success in the markets we were trying to reach. Our strategic insight was completely right, but our execution was flawed.

My preferred option here is either to acquire or to build businesses or bits of businesses, within the core, and then spin them out when they reach a meaningful size. This was exactly what Lou Gerstner did with IBM's services business, which sat inside their sales operation until it reached the appropriate scale to sit as a unit within IBM.

In the short term, this caused enormous conflict – as the hardware sales people and the services teams fought like cats and dogs. At the *Guardian*, this is what we did with a range of events, supplements and education businesses that we eventually put under one brand (Guardian Professional) which, as I have mentioned, now makes a significant contribution to the business.

The innovation unit: lessons from Apollo 13 and *The Economist*

What we really need is an innovation unit! You know we need to get some of our best people to work on some cool stuff, step away from their day jobs, have a bit of dedicated resource, and do some blue sky thinking. You know – we need to. If it doesn't work – we can just kill it; but if it flies, we could come up with the next Twitter.

This isn't a direct quote from anyone in particular – but I have heard variations from people in all sorts of businesses. The initial assumption is right. It is teeth-grindingly difficult to get smart innovative projects off the ground within big organisations. There is always a more urgent and important call on resource. No matter how you shuffle things round, small smart ideas always end up stuck at the bottom of the to-do list, normally shunted out of the way for big stupid ones that the business, unfortunately, happens to depend on.

❝ internal innovation units can and do work ❞

Internal innovation units can and do work. They are particularly useful in coming up with the products and processes that will help with a core transformation – as we will see with the example of British Airways below. But, what matters is that giving a team freedom to innovate is not the same as giving them freedom. In fact, I believe the reverse often leads to better results.

My favourite example of an innovation project comes from the Apollo 13 mission – America's equivalent of Dunkirk, a triumph of survival in the face of disaster. Everything went horribly wrong on the mission when one of the astronauts, Jack Swigert, caused an explosion while stirring the oxygen tanks, and the three-man crew had to move into the two-man lunar landing module, Aquarius, to get them home.

The problem with having three men in a two-man capsule was that they were creating too much carbon dioxide. If something wasn't done to filter the gas it would poison all the astronauts before they landed. Back in Houston, an engineering team was put together with all the materials that the astronauts have at their disposal in their craft. They had a few hours to use them to create an effective filter. The pressure was on, and the stakes were high. Eventually, they came up with a neat adapter to use with the command module's air filters in the Aquarius. They then explained to the astronauts exactly how to build it and, as a result, everyone was saved.

There are four reasons I think this provides a good role model for internal innovation:

■ there was a very clear problem to solve
■ there was no doubt about the importance of the problem
■ there was complete clarity about the time and resource available
■ they didn't just solve the problem – they made sure the solution was implemented on the spaceship.

The human mind does its best work when it is solving problems, not simply staring into space looking at opportunities or trying to 'come up with ideas'. A problem provides focus, and success is simple: you solve it, or you don't. When you speak to successful entrepreneurs about where they got the idea for their business from, you'll often find that it came about as a solution to a problem that they, or their friends or relatives, had.

Internal innovation projects all too often fail to meet these four criteria. The potential list of things to do is too vast, but none of them have any real importance or urgency. As a result, there is an endless process of comparing apples and oranges as you try to decide what you should focus your efforts on. Even if you manage to deliver something, you have simply created a new dilemma: what is the business actually going to do with it?

In 2007, *The Economist* launched Project Red Stripe, giving six staff six months and £100,000 to come up with 'the next big thing'. They put some of their smartest and most digitally savvy people on to it, who were all taken away from day-to-day responsibilities and given a completely blank canvas in order to develop new business ideas.

It failed. A description of the whole project by Andrew Carey, an author who observed the process, gives you a pretty much perfect description about how not to do things. Perhaps most important of all, too much time was spent discussing what they were actually trying to do. The freedom they had craved became something of a curse.

From the outset, the Red Stripe team sometimes 'wandered around' without a clear sense of what was going to happen next and without any clarity as to how to make things happen. Instinctively, drifting seems like an appropriate thing for an innovation team to do; but it's also an uncomfortable and anxiety-inducing thing to do. Some say that safety is a prerequisite of creativity, and there were certainly some members of the Red Stripe team who worked hardest and fastest when they knew where they were going.[1]

They came up with some neat ideas, but nothing that was implemented – and as a result, they failed to either transform the way they worked day to day or open up a big opportunity.[2]

The *Guardian*'s new media lab, that I walked into way back in 1996, was a large version of Project Red Stripe: smart, but somewhat rudderless. We did lots of 'cool' things, and yes – we made some pretty

---

1 Andrew Carey (2008) *Inside Project Red Stripe*, Triarchy Press.
2 For a full inside account of Project Red Stripe read the project's blog: http://projectredstripe.blogspot.com/

good money, but it was too random, and too much a celebration of our own cleverness. The department only sprang to life and became truly useful when we focused on the core task of defining what the newspaper's online presence should be.

Being on the edge of the business gave us the right amount of freedom we needed to decide, for example, that we would respond to news as it happened throughout the day, rather than simply wait for that evening's copy from the paper (a radical move at the time). The support and high expectations of our editor, Alan Rusbridger, and managing director, Carolyn McCall, left us under the clear impression that this was important. Constant competitive activity in the market left us in no doubt about the urgency.

Tips for setting up an innovation unit

1 Give them a clear and important problem to solve – a broken process in the business, or an underperforming product, or a set of customers whose needs you're no longer meeting. Place a value on the solution: is this a $1m problem? A $100m problem?

2 Resource and time have to be finite – but make sure they have enough of both to test a number of solutions to the problem.

3 Create risk, reward and competition. Give the same problem to two or more teams. If the problem has a significant value, then they deserve a significant reward for solving it.

4 Most important of all remind them that it's not enough to make it work in the artificial confines of their project. Just like the air filter in Apollo 13 they also have to get it to work on the mothership.

Open innovation

'Open innovation' has become one of the more favoured buzzwords in recent years. In his book, *Open Innovation: The new imperative for creating and profiting from technology*, Berkeley professor Henry

Chesbrough describes it as 'a paradigm that assumes that firms can and should use external ideas as well as internal ideas, and internal and external paths to market.' In other words – rather than simply putting all your smartest people in a room to solve a problem, you simply put the problem out on the internet, and let the world come up with the solution.

Probably the most perfect example of this happened in 2006, when Netflix offered $1m to anyone who could improve the quality of the recommendations on their site by 10%. What seemed like a pretty straightforward challenge turned out to involve three years of global collaboration and mathematical prowess. Individuals working on the problem start to work together as teams. Teams merged to pool their work. In September 2009, they finally awarded the prize to the team BellKor's Pragmatic Chaos. The $1m prize was eye catching – but, the man hours that went into solving the problem would have cost Netflix many, many times that if they had paid for them on the open market. And, as a PR initiative, it was worth it for the global coverage the award received.

> **❝ the $1m prize was eye catching ❞**

The point about open innovation is that when it works well, as with the Netflix Prize, it does so because it follows many of the same rules for innovation units set out above (see the box) – a clear and important problem to solve, and a measurable definition of success. Not only that, but right from the outset, as those solving the problem work from live Netflix data, the solution is ready to integrate with the core business.

Netflix is a big enough name to do something like this by themselves, and attract attention all by themselves. Other businesses, however, might not have a $1m problem to solve – and might not be fantastically well known. This is where an operation like Innocentive steps in. They have created an 'open innovation marketplace' where anyone can post a problem – normally a scientific or engineering one – with a clearly stated reward for solving it; and throw it open to the community of academics, enthusiastic amateurs and organisations looking for a bit of extra revenue.

Cisco approaches open innovation in a different way. It holds an annual iPrize, where anyone from around the world can put forward an idea for a new business. Initial proposals are then refined over a period of months – people can collaborate or comment on each other's proposals – and the best idea ultimately wins a prize of $250,000, in exchange for which Cisco gets to license the idea. The only limit is that the ideas must fall under one of four broad headings: The Future of Work, The Connected Life, New Ways to Learn, and The Future of Entertainment.

I like the Cisco prize – time will tell if it delivers successful businesses as well as column inches of good publicity and access to some very smart young brains who might go on to become future Cisco executives. But, if we are looking at open innovation that really hits the spot, I prefer the tightly defined problem solving of the Netflix Prize. That way, great work lies.

Transform the core by innovating at the edges – the relaunch of BA.com

Simon Talling-Smith joined the British Airways graduate trainee scheme straight after graduating in engineering from Oxford. He rose swiftly through the ranks, and in 2001, while in his early 30s, he was made BA's head of e-commerce, and given the task of sorting out their rather chaotic online presence. The way he tackled this challenge, I believe, gives as great an example of how a separate 'innovation unit' should be used to help transform a core business.

When he was given the challenge, there was, he recalls, a lot of online activity, but not much direction. 'We were throwing everything at it, and it looked like it.'[3] There was a general sense that they had to 'do'

---

3 This and subsequent quotes are from interviews with the author.

e-commerce because everyone else was. It was very much an adjunct to the business – and as such viewed suspiciously by many around the organisation who had seen the dotcom bubble burst, and felt that the internet was really just hype.

His breakthrough was to stop thinking about the internet as another distinct channel, but rather as a way to use it to change the way that consumers engaged with British Airways, and in turn to change the way that BA operated. It was a transformation at the very core of their business.

Talling-Smith and his team started by listening to consumers – and heard what they knew, deep down to be true: airlines were difficult to deal with. There was horrific opaqueness about pricing. Everyone complained that they would see a cheap flight advertised on a bus-side and then phone up the airline or go to their website and there would be no sign of it. Customers also felt the need to work with travel agents – who again, added another layer of opacity to the whole process of simply booking a flight.

The common wisdom within the business though is that obfuscation was good for them. Confusion meant people relied on intermediaries, and paid more than they had to for their seats. 'We made a margin out of opaqueness,' said Talling-Smith. But in an era of cheap flights – this kind of behaviour wasn't going to work.

In other words, his open-ended task rapidly turned into a set of consistent problems to be solved and led to an overall vision for the e-commerce business. The aim was not to 'build a great website' but 'to make BA so easy to do business with that customers would choose to do it themselves'.

The next crucial part of the programme was to turn it into a way to take cost out of the business by making it simpler and more efficient. The team estimated – and now Talling-Smith admits it was nothing more than an estimate – that they could take £100m from the fixed cost base, and this could be achieved with a £25m investment. And that secured sign off from the board.

That figure sounds huge, but to put this in context, at the time BA had a cost base of around £8bn. That year it was embarking on a reduction in its property portfolio, which it was planning to reduce by £600m. In other words, while £100m is a large amount of anyone's money, it was not on its own a game-changer for a business the size of BA. But it was enough to make the whole exercise meaningful for the board, and therefore make it a key strategic initiative for the business.

> **❝ there were no private offices, and very few desks, there were long 'farmhouse tables' for teams ❞**

The project took over a floor at BA's headquarters – with 100 project managers from around the company moving in. It was done out completely differently to any other BA office space. There were no private offices, and very few desks, instead there were long 'farmhouse tables' for teams to sit around.

Talling-Smith himself didn't use a desk – choosing instead to sit with a different team every week. If you have worked in a start-up, or an organisation with a flat structure, or a great nature of openness, none of these things would sound particularly remarkable. In the British Airways of 2002, however, it was practically revolutionary.

The project was also run differently to anything else that normally happened within British Airways. One of Talling-Smith's direct reports was called the 'venture capitalist' and each sub-project had to secure funding from him; and they were only ever given funding for three months of activity.

At the same time, Talling-Smith established the principle of rapid secondments. People were brought in from different units around BA, but only to work for three months. After this, they went back to their team – energised, and convincing everyone back in their own unit of just how important the e-business project was. They were half way between evangelists and sleeper agents, embedded all the way through the organisation. This created a sense of nimbleness and urgency around the whole project. But, more importantly, it blurred the lines between the core of the business and the team that was squirrelled away on the fourth floor, that was about to change the way that many of them worked.

Too often with an internal programme, you hear tales of a 'them and us' culture – a fundamental split and resentment between those working on the new cool thing, and those who are focused on the thing that currently brings in all the money. I have no doubt there was some of that dynamic within BA, but what is clear that Talling-Smith was doing his best to minimise it right from the start. This was vital because even though the team was driving the project, it still needed to work with the rest of BA in order to make it happen.

Take for example the development of the Fare Explorer. This took an idea from budget airlines that was completely counter to the 'making a margin from opaqueness' strategy that BA had previously adopted.

It allowed anyone looking to book a flight to see not just the price on the days they wanted to travel, but also the different prices if they decided to fly on different days and at different times, with colour coding to make it even easier. Making this work technically was one issue, but getting it accepted within the business required working tightly with the pricing and sales teams – not always with their blessing. Talling-Smith recalls:

I remember one of the senior pricing guys saying to me: 'Look, Simon, if you show people these low prices, they might actually buy them … I had to remind him that the reason the prices were low is that we needed to sell them.'[4]

The other big initiative was the introduction of both e-tickets and being able to check in before you arrived at the airport. Both of which hit the innovation sweet-spot of making consumers' lives easier while taking out a raft of cost and complexity in both printing and processing tickets and boarding cards.

The end result was that British Airways saved the £100m that the

---

4 In an interview with the author.

project set out to do. (The actual sum was £102m.) Call centres were closed as sales went online; and payments to agents were reduced as customers went direct. The business became just that bit simpler – both internally and externally. Most importantly, it made the airline a better business to deal with.

Has this programme secured BA's permanent well being? Not at all – they continue to face a host of challenges. But Talling-Smith's approach, I believe, offers a set of very clear lessons for anyone who is just about to set up a smart innovation unit in order to help transform their core business.

Lessons from the BA.com revamp

- **The need for a meaningful prize:** a £100m saving was the right incentive at the right time for the board to support the initiative.

- **Put a star in charge:** Talling-Smith was clearly one of BA's rising stars. He fits my 'rockstar' category perfectly. He now runs their Americas operation. Having him in charge acted as a magnet for talent elsewhere in the business; and a signal to those within the business that this was a key project.

- **Improving the consumer experience + saving cost = transformation nirvana.** Simply cutting cost will only take a business so far. Doing so, while you are becoming a better business for customers to deal with is God's own work. We should all strive to achieve such a thing.

- **The critical need to engage with the business:** Talling-Smith's policy of rapid secondments meant he was creating a network of evangelists throughout the business. They proved vital when it came to securing support from marketing, pricing and sales teams.

- **Keep the energy levels up throughout the programme:** by reviewing all funding on a three-month basis, and constantly rotating staff, BA kept momentum going throughout.

Corporate venturing

'Why don't we just take a stake in ...'

The final area I want to look at in this theme of edge innovations is the world of corporate venturing – or taking minority stakes in start-up businesses. For a variety of reasons, doing this well is much harder than it seems. Research from Ashridge Business School in the UK has shown that 'less than five per cent of corporate venture efforts create value'.[5]

Part of the problem is that corporate venturing tends to spike at exactly the wrong time – when the market and valuations are at their highest – and then venturers get out when the market is at its lowest. And as even an amateur investor will know, you should really be doing things the other way round.

According to data from the National Venture Capital Association,[6] for example, corporate venturing's share of investment rose to around 16% of the venture market during the boom of 2000 and then fell to around 6–8% of the market during 2002–03, which was when the first seeds of the Web 2.0 boom were being sowed. As the market picked up again – and valuations along with it – so the corporate venturers came back into the market. And sure enough, by the first half of 2007, with a new web boom under way, corporate venturers were on the rise again – up to 9% of all VC funding.

“ the corporate venturers came back into the market ”

In other words, there is a strong tendency for corporate venturers to buy at the top of the market. Furthermore, the precise reasons for a lot of corporate venture activity indicate that 50% of investors are investing 'primarily for strategic reasons, but financial return is a

5 Julian Birkinshaw and Andrew Campbell (2004) 'Know the Limits of Corporate Venturing', *Financial Times*, 9 August.
6 National Venture Capital Association, Corporate Venture Capital: Seeking Innovation and Strategic Growth, 2008.

requirement', 15% are investing for 'strategic reasons only' and the same amount are investing for 'financial reasons only'.[7]

And this, I believe, gets us to the nub of the matter. It is very tempting when a smart start-up comes to your door and asks for a relatively small amount of cash in exchange for a strategic stake. But as with every other initiative we have looked at, you have to ask 'why?' and, just as importantly, 'what are you going to do next?'

Hiding behind the broad heading of 'strategic reasons' I'm afraid simply isn't good enough – as with every other aspect of innovation discussed in this section, you are either doing it because you believe it will help you transform your core business, or because it will nudge you in the right direction for a big adjacency.

There are very sound financial reasons behind corporate venturing as opposed to either acquiring or developing a business organically. Most important of all for businesses that have to deliver constant earnings growth, it gives you access to smart start-ups and innovation, without having to carry any loss on your P&L. However, building up a portfolio of small stakes in interesting businesses takes time and effort – and can prove to be massively diversionary if it is done incorrectly or for the wrong purposes. And just as those within big businesses often aren't the best entrepreneurs, they're also not necessarily the best venture capitalists. The skill of doing the right deal at the right time is one that has to be learned.

So what works? And how should you do it? Of all the businesses I have spoken to about this, the two companies I think that offer the approaches most worth replicating are Disney and WPP.

Disney

Disney has a separate venture operation called the Steamboat Fund. It is run by John Ball, who had experience of working within Disney's

---

7 Ibid.

finance unit, but also experience of working within a VC fund. Steamboat has been cautious with its investments: the fund was launched in 2000 and after ten years, they have only taken stakes in some 30 businesses even after setting up a separate fund focused on China.

They focus primarily on technology businesses in the media and entertainment sector that deliver the sort of products and services that Disney would never develop organically, but which might be critical to their future. A handful of senior Disney executives sits on the investment committee – which means that they see the sort of businesses and opportunities that are coming into their markets.

The stakes are in the region of $2m–$15m; and once the investment has been made, they will act as a door opener – introducing the business to the relevant bits of Disney. However, there is nothing promised. Most importantly of all though, this is ultimately run as a fund. Investments are made with a view to a financial return – even though the absolute scale of the investments is slight in comparison to Disney as a whole. The discipline is vital.

WPP

At WPP, Mark Read, the director of strategy, runs a unit, WPP Digital, that makes acquisitions and takes strategic stakes in the digital start-ups that they believe are going to transform the world of marketing services.

The unit was set up in 2005, and it has built up some 20 stakes in different businesses, as well as the major acquisition of 24/7 Real Media. Their investments include the likes of WildTangent, which specialises in online games, and Visible Technologies, which offers social media monitoring.

In all cases, Read's criteria for investing are that they can help them grow, and WPP has good visibility of the market they operate in. Furthermore, they always make their investments with a VC alongside them. Once the investments are made, then Read and his team make a deliberate effort to get them working with the agencies and clients around WPP.

Differences in approach

There are slight differences between Disney and WPP's approach. Disney's is much more of a pure investment vehicle and that is a matter of corporate preference more than anything else. But in both cases, there are similar disciplines for investment.

- There is a rich seam of potential investments that would never be delivered organically: both WPP and Disney find themselves in markets where technology has an ever greater impact, but neither of them are technology companies. In other words, there isn't much debate about 'buy or build' as there is almost no chance that the companies they are investing in would come organically from their organisations.

- This is a centralised activity. Even in organisations the size of Disney and WPP you don't have different businesses doing different things. In other words, when start-ups come knocking at the door, there is a place for them to be sent to, and a set process for them to be dealt with.

- There is a 'trusted' executive in charge. Read is WPP's overall head of strategy and works closely with Sir Martin Sorrell. Ball came from Disney's finance team. Both men have credibility both at their corporate centre and around their operating businesses: which is vital to get the most out of the individual investments.

- There is a deliberate effort to get the investments working with business units – but no promise that it will happen.

- Both Steamboat and WPP Digital are trusted parts of the investment community. This is critical. Just as WPP and Disney need to find companies they want to invest in, start-ups need to believe that taking on WPP and Disney as investors is a good decision. Similarly, other investors need to know that having them on board will help rather than harm their chances of a good exit.

8

Putting it all together: Kodak's long road back

Consider this: The average Chinese household takes fewer than 18 pictures a year – less than half a roll of 36-exposure film. But when the average Chinese household starts using one whole roll of film a year, it will be like adding another entire market the size of Germany... We believe that in perhaps ten years, China could become the world's largest picture market. (George Fisher, Kodak CEO, 1995)[1]

In two or three years, this will be seen as one of the most successful transformations in the history of our country. (Antonio Perez, Kodak CEO, 2007)[2]

If there is a single business that has helped to shape my thinking while researching this book, it has been Eastman Kodak. Many years ago, I noticed a raft of similarities between Kodak and the newspaper industry: justifiable pride in their past achievements; a sense of real importance about what their business does that went beyond pure financial returns; an era of spectacular financial growth, and then profound disruption – brought on ultimately (but not exclusively) by the dawn of the digital world.

---

1 Quoted in 'Kodak's New Focus', *Business Week*, 13 February 1995.
2 Quoted in *Business Week* in 2007, http://businessweek.com/magazine/content/06_48/b4011421.htm

❝ Kodak's core photography business has revenues of less than $500m ❞

Creative disruption for Kodak has been particularly brutal. Fifteen years on from the quote by George Fisher above, the business that he was hoping to see grow across the globe is now a shadow of its former self. Total revenues are down from around $15bn to below $8bn. The company has eaten up cash as earnings have reduced and there has been wave after wave of restructuring costs. Staff numbers have been reduced by some 80%, and the share price has dropped by around 90%. Kodak's consumer film business, which used to generate some $10bn in annual revenues and the majority of their profits, now has revenues of less than $500m.

And this at a time, of course, when we take more photographs than at any time in human history. In the mid 1990s there were 450 million people with cameras. Now there are hundreds of millions of smart phones and digital cameras out there – with people snapping away like never before. 'Photography' has boomed, Kodak has crumbled. But, it has survived. It is still has one of the most recognised brands in the world; and Antonio Perez has given the company focus and strategic clarity, even though the business in 2010 has been battered by both the accelerated decline of film and the recession. Over four quarters from the end of 2008, the business's cumulative losses ran to $1.4bn, only finally breaking into profit at the end of 2009 thanks to some one-off licensing payments.

The Eastman Kodak that Perez runs is not simply a shrunken version of the one that Fisher took over, it is a completely different business, and has undergone exactly the sort of reinvention we have talked about in the previous chapters. It has a different set of products, and different set of divisions, operates in different markets, and employs different people. In 2009, 60% of Kodak employees had been with the business for less than four years – in a business where employees would work for decades, often following their parents into the business, this kind of renewal is nothing short of spectacular.

The story of Kodak over the past 20 years provides enough material for a book of its own, and it is dangerous to over-simplify it. Over the years, I have heard dozens of suggestions for what Kodak should have done – pretty much all of which ignore what the various executive teams actually *did* over the years and fail to take into account that this was a $10bn publicly owned company, employing (at one point) more than a 100,000 staff and in need of complete reinvention, not a $2m start-up in need of a management away day.

But, I want to focus on three phases of the Kodak story. First is the late 1980s and early 1990s when the business first started to run into trouble. Next we'll look at Kodak under George Fisher, the 'rockstar' CEO brought into the business to turn it around in 1993. Fisher did a lot of good things, but ultimately failed to make the company fit for a digital future. Finally, we will jump to Kodak going into 2010 – and some of the things they appear to be doing right. If Perez is to be believed, the reinvented Kodak is a platform for 'sustainable profitable growth'. If he is right, then the quote at the start of this chapter – that this is going to be one of the great transformations – will not be far off the mark. If he is wrong, however, we are witnessing the final instalments of one of the greatest slow motion car crashes in corporate history. It can still go either way.

Finally, looking at our three themes of core transformation, finding big adjacencies and edge innovations, we'll see how things might have panned out differently.

Pre-1993: the seeds of decline, sown in growth

For much of the 20th century, Kodak's film business wasn't just a good business, it was a great business. Kodak won three times with every photo you took: once when you took the photo on your Kodak film, a second time when you had it developed with Kodak chemicals, and then when you had it printed on Kodak paper. Their operating margins here were around 60% and one Kodak manager pointed out that it was difficult to think of anything that was legal with similar profit margins to colour photography!

This was a massive, vertically integrated, global business. Kodak were used to doing everything themselves – at one stage they even farmed their own cows to create the gelatin needed to make films. They had research labs that secured scores of patents; and the beating heart of the business was its massive manufacturing plant, Kodak Park, in their home town of Rochester in upstate New York. This was a production line not only for their films, chemicals and paper, but also for most of the senior executives within the business.

However, it had become clear in the mid- to late-1980s that their position in the film market was going to be massively challenged. The problem at that time wasn't so much the looming threat of digital cameras, but immediate competition from low-cost and own-brand films. The biggest, and most direct threat, came from Fuji – which had come from nowhere in the late 1970s to take around 20% global share in 1993.

Fuji didn't just offer cheaper film and paper, it also brought successful innovations to the market, introducing the 400-speed film and the single-use camera (something that Kodak had developed in its labs, but failed to patent). Facing up to the decline in their core film business, Kodak started to look for big adjacencies.

Building on their strength in the chemicals market, Kodak started to buy their way into life sciences and pharmaceuticals. The biggest move here was the $5.1bn purchase of Sterling Whitmore Healthcare in 1988 and with it the creation of Eastman Pharmaceuticals division. But these moves left them with nearly $8bn in debt, placing massive strain on the film business to generate the cash to pay down the debt.

At the same time, Kodak started to make moves into digital imaging and data storage. Some of this came through acquisitions – buying IBM's photocopying business for example – but the business also embarked on masses of R&D in this area. They had developed the first digital camera in 1975 and the first image sensor in 1986. They also set up an electronic photography division in 1987. In other words, they didn't ignore the digital world – but they did have difficulties bringing winning product to market, and in general in thinking like a digital business.

John White, an executive who joined the business in 1988 said:

Kodak wanted to get into the digital business, but they wanted to do it in their own way, from Rochester and largely with their own people. That meant it wasn't going to work. The difference between their traditional business and digital is so great. The tempo is different, the kind of skills you need are different. Kay [Whitmore, CEO] ... would tell you they wanted change, but they didn't want to force the pain on the organisation.[3]

The fear of cannibalisation was a powerful and understandable force within the business. Why kill off your 60% margin business for one that might at best, they thought, bring in 15% margins? Digital imaging threatened to completely undermine Kodak's holy trinity of film, chemicals and paper, and for a generation of executives brought up through Kodak, there was no good that could come from this particular innovation.

A friend of a friend tells me a story of a meeting he had with some middle managers at Kodak during this era. 'What are you going to do about digital photography?' he asked them at the

❝ Kodak still saw digital development through a film-shaped prism ❞

end of the meeting. 'Drive it back into the water,' was their reply. Even when they weren't displaying Canute-like resistance, Kodak still saw digital development through a film-shaped prism. The broad vision for 'digital' developed at first within Kodak was for 'film-based digital imaging' – we would start by taking photos on film and then have them developed into digital formats.

This lay behind the 1991 launch of the Photo CD system in partnership with Philips. This was a $500 box that allowed you to play photos taken on film and then digitised in a lab and burnt onto a proprietary

---

3 Quoted in Alecia Swasy (1998) *Changing Focus: Kodak and the Battle to Save a Great American Company*, Random House.

format CD, through your TV. The discs each cost $20. It was meant to be a $600m business with $100m of operating earnings. It flopped.

But perhaps the biggest challenge of all lay with Eastman Kodak as an organisation – and the fact that after 50 years of dominating its market, it had become unfit to deal with rapid change and fierce competition.

Yes, they had a phenomenal brand, and a place in the heart of the American psyche. And, yes, even after Fuji had stolen share off them year after year, they were both global and domestic market leader by some way. But decades of success had made them increasingly hierarchical and unwieldy. They were, as Peter Nulty said in *Fortune* magazine, 'one of the most bureaucratic, wasteful, paternalistic, slow-moving, isolated, and beloved companies in America'.[4]

Trying to fix this took time, effort and money. By 1993, the company had undergone five restructurings in a decade; and run up some $2.4bn in restructuring charges over three years. Over the past 15 years those restructuring costs have continued to pile up and take cash out of the business. The medicine wasn't working. The debt taken on from the wave of acquisitions was crippling the business, and so the board brought in a new chief executive – the first from outside the company, George Fisher of Motorola.

Before we look at Fisher's era, it's worth taking stock. Because within the pre-1993 era we see the seeds of the problems that would continue to challenge Kodak for the next 15 years.

The seeds of the problem

Transforming the core

To put it simply – there wasn't enough done here quickly enough, and this would remain a theme for the next decade. Kodak's

---

4 Peter Nulty (1994) 'Kodak Grabs for Growth Again', *Fortune*, 16 May, pp. 76–78.

dominant era in film was coming to an end, and there was competition mounting on all sides.

Digital photography was still some years away from the mass market. But, there was a real and pressing need to make the film business competitive in the face of the onslaught from Fuji.

A good comparator from earlier in the book is Deutsche Post. Their great reinvention happened not in the face of the internet, but with the looming spectre of privatisation and increased competition. The result was a radical and profound transformation of their core mail business; which, in the end, made them much more resilient for the structural decline that the internet would later bring to them.

Finding big adjacencies

The whole of the Kodak story might have been different if the move into life sciences and pharmaceuticals had been managed better. This, and only this, was the only move that might have allowed Kodak the potential for sustained growth through the digital-driven disruption that would follow. Here was a sector that carried with it growth potential, had high barriers to entry, and built on their R&D and manufacturing capabilities in chemical technology.

But, it didn't work out. Sterling wasn't the right company and they paid too much for it, saddling the business with debt on the way.

Innovating at the edges

Kodak was proud of its R&D, and they had been very active in their pursuit of digital photography in their labs. But there was a disconnection between this and bringing successful products to market. The Photo CD system can go on the great scrap-pile of failed consumer technologies of the early 1990s. More worrying was letting Fuji steal ground with the arrival of 400 ASA film and disposable cameras.

Throughout this period, there was no shortage of patents being filed by Kodak, not least in the digital imaging area. But, this wasn't fuelling a fundamental strategic drive to transform the business into a digital business. The fear of cannibalisation meant that great ideas remained in the labs.

The point here is that being 'innovative' was no longer enough. The challenge was to focus that innovation into bringing winning products to market as quickly as possible. And this would be at the heart of George Fisher's plan.

Enter George Fisher: rockstar CEO

George Fisher joined Eastman Kodak in 1993 following a hugely successful stint in running Motorola. He was the first outsider brought in to run the company and his hire was a major coup for Kodak. He had previously turned down the job at IBM later taken up by Lou Gerstner. The two men's experiences during the years from 1993–2000 provide an interesting comparison. While Gerstner, as we have read, left behind him a transformed IBM that has since become a powerhouse in software and services, Fisher left at the end of 1999 with Kodak still grappling with many of the demons of the previous era.

Fisher did a lot of the right things at Kodak. He rapidly set about changing a business that was riddled with bureaucracy and hierarchy. He created a culture of accountability where previously obfuscation and buck-passing had reigned supreme. And Fisher's personal style was different to anything Kodak employees had seen from their previous senior leaders: he ate breakfast in the canteen and personally responded to staff e-mails (admittedly he did this by having them printed out by his assistant and then handwriting a response, but even that was a radical leap forward).

ff Fisher's personal style was different ᴊᴊ

The Economist reported on the change programme that Fisher was putting into place in the middle of 1994. It describes the classic urgency and change that follows the arrival of a new broom, sweeping through the business.

Ten teams of senior managers – two of them led by Mr. Fisher – have been charged with rethinking everything from product development to how to expand Kodak's markets. R&D which, according to Mike Morley, head of human resources, used to be 'a confused process at best' is being more tightly organised. Throughout the company the talk is of cross-functional teams, parallel product development and compressed cycle times.[5]

Fisher swiftly sorted out the debt problem by selling off the pharmaceutical businesses – at a loss. Instead of attempts to diversify, he focused the business on imaging: but made it clear that this went beyond the traditional world of film, chemicals and paper: 'We are not in the photographic film business or in the electronics business,' he said, 'we are in the picture business'.[6]

At Motorola, Fisher had grown to understand the importance and practices of the Chinese market. He brought this experience with him to Kodak, offering the hope of significant growth in the film market. He pointed out that half of the world was yet to take a picture and 'The opportunity is huge,' he said, 'and it's nothing fancy. We just have to sell yellow boxes of film.'[7]

Beyond film, Fisher got the company to start taking digital imaging seriously. He found that Kodak had spent some $5bn on R&D in digital imaging, but its efforts were scattered and fragmented, and slow to come to market. At one stage there were 23 different digital scanner projects. He brought the digital efforts together into a Digital and Applied Imaging Division and brought in Carl Gustin, an executive who had previously worked at DEC and Apple, to run it. Gustin and his team started whittling down the time it took to get products to market, and the business started to work with the likes of Apple, Microsoft and Sun to become part of the digital world.

But in the summer of 1997, disaster struck. The business found itself in a knife fight on their home turf when Fuji started a price war in the domestic market. The price war with Fuji wasn't just a local issue of

5 'Picture Imperfect', *The Economist*, 28 May 1994.
6 Address to the Academy of Management, Boston, August 1997 and quoted in Robert M. Grant's excellent case study of Kodak (case 6) in *Cases in Contemporary Strategy Analysis* by R.M. Grant and K.E. Neupert (2003, Blackwell).
7 Ibid.

dealing with a competitor, it was elevated into an international trade issue as Kodak tried to break down the barriers that prevented it from getting into the Japanese market. Fisher accused Fuji of using the cash from their protected domestic market to allow predatory pricing in the US. This was war.

Meanwhile Fuji started to build a state-of-the-art production plant for photographic paper – threatening to further swamp a market where there was already no shortage of capacity. There were problems too with the launch of a new film format: APS. Kodak had spent some $500m on this, but there were problems with distribution and consumers didn't really understand why they should be using it. For a company used to introducing new formats and seeing profits soar as a result, this was yet another wake-up call. To rub salt into the wound, Fuji – who had launched with the same format at the same time – seemed to be having reasonable success with it.

As a final blow, the digital businesses weren't making any money. Fisher was spending about $500m a year on research and product development. Cameras and scanners were churning out of their factories at a very reasonable rate of knots, and sales of digital imaging products were rising – at around 25% a year. But this wasn't profitable and in 1997 the loss from the digital imaging business came in at around $200m.

The problem with the consumer digital business is that Kodak found itself competing against HP, Epson, Sony, and a host of others, and the margins were meagre. No sooner was a digital camera launched than along came another one with a higher spec and a lower price. There were also signs that the growth of digital imaging was leading to even greater disruption than imagined. Fisher had placed his bet on people going to a shop to get their digital images printed out through a Kodak kiosk, but consumers were starting to buy cheap inkjet printers to print at home. While Kodak grappled with thinking about how it could get into the home printing market, HP, Canon and Epson all moved right in and took it.

As a result of all this, sales, earnings and revenue had all stalled. The share price, that had welcomed Fisher's arrival, had started to fall back. Meanwhile, the cost base was still too big.

❝ sales, earnings and revenue had all stalled ❞

Nearly 30,000 jobs had gone when they exited the healthcare business, but at the end of 1996, the number of employees in continuing operations had actually gone up by 3,000 to around 95,000. Operating costs as a percentage of sales were around 27.6% – the same as they were when Fisher arrived.

Fisher's initial efforts, however, might have initially impressed, but they didn't deliver sustainable benefits. The business lost share in the US to Fuji and operating earnings fell by 24% as a result. By the middle of 2007, some four years after he took the job, it became clear that he had to be more decisive, and deliver the sort of cuts that Wall Street had been asking for all along – the sort of cuts, indeed, that Lou Gerstner had introduced at IBM.

Fisher ordered $1bn in cost reductions over two years. He sacked the heads of the three most critical businesses, cut 200 managers and 16,000 other jobs; and slashed more than $100m from the $1bn R&D budget. It was dramatic, but it should have happened much sooner. As analyst Eugene Glazer commented at the time: 'Fisher moved too slowly and didn't instil a sense of urgency.' The result, he added, was 'a serious credibility problem'.[8]

Why the delay? There was a fair amount of denial throughout the business. Most notably there was still a belief that consumers would stick to taking pictures on film for years to come – even though they would increasingly have them then converted to digital images for storage.

Some of this no doubt came from a reasonable underestimation of just how quickly consumers would switch to digital. But it also came from the fact that the digital business was losing hundreds of millions

8 Quoted in 'Why Kodak Still Isn't Fixed', Linda Grant, *Fortune*, 11 May 1988.

a year, and the idea that this was going to provide a commercial replacement for film was not financially credible.

'If we think our past was film, and our future is digital, we're going to have problems,'[9] said Fisher. He was right. They were going to have problems.

Fisher left Kodak in December 2000 – just as the real damage was about to happen to the film business, and digital camera sales were about to soar. His sidekick and ultimate successor, Daniel Carp, had to make even more cuts as he grappled with the stagnation and then decline of film sales and an economic downturn.

Fisher did many good things at Kodak. When I hear blandishments about 'what Kodak should have done', the answers are almost always things that George Fisher actually did. But none of this was enough.

As James Surowiecki commented in the online magazine *Slate* the day after Fisher resigned:

It's one thing to clean up a company's balance sheet and make it leaner and more efficient. It's another to restore it to long-term health. You could say that Kodak's continued mediocre performance is just proof that Fisher wasn't 'the right guy'. He certainly did not do an ideal job, but it's more likely that Kodak just wasn't the right place.[10]

Perhaps the task was just too great for any chief executive to achieve.

Fisher's work was always going to be cut out. Even after the balance sheet had been sorted out, the combination of a fear of cannibalisation still ran through the business. There was both denial and delusion about the potential for the film market (although that was not Kodak's fault alone). The transformation of the core business was too slow and there was no big adjacency to move into.

All of the four killer mindsets seem to have been at play here: a denial about the impact of digital; a delusion about customers' fondness for film, and Kodak's ability to maintain its premium pricing; distraction

---

9 Ibid.
10 James Surowiecki (1999) 'The Limits of CEO Magic', *Slate*, 10 June.

from the price war with Fuji; and ultimately bewilderment as the challenges just mounted and mounted.

If one thing could have changed Fisher's tenancy it might have been a visit from the ghost of Christmas future – showing him the average American family in 2010, snapping photos on their iPhones, sharing them over the internet on Flickr, or using their digital cameras and putting them on Facebook and only printing out the odd one on their home inkjet printer: an entire value chain of digital imaging with Kodak playing only the slightest role. I suspect that that, and only that, would have resulted in a different outcome. Even the price war with Fuji would have seemed like small beer; and I suspect much more radical steps would have to be taken much earlier.

Fisher vs Gerstner

Gerstner succeeded where Fisher failed for two reasons – first he tackled the process of core transformation head on. He took out 35,000 jobs within two years, dramatically reducing the cost base at every opportunity. Faced with a price war in the mainframe market, and seeing competitors selling at 30% less then IBM, he radically reinvented the mainframe, and bought it an extra lease of life through the CMOS chip (which allowed them to lower their prices and operate at the same gross margin).

Gerstner also made sure that he didn't simply move into the market that was destroying the mainframe business – namely the PC market. This rapidly became a commodity market, just like mid-to-low range digital cameras, scanners and inkjet printers that provided the focus of much of Kodak's first wave of digital product development. IBM moved to the professional market of services and software, just as Kodak would increasingly move a third of its business into high-end printing and imaging services.

2010 and beyond

Antonio Perez was brought over from Hewlett Packard where he had been head of the consumer division to be President and COO under Daniel Carp in 2003. He was then promoted to replace Carp as Chair and CEO in 2005. And how have the first five years gone? The ongoing narrative has been about the crashing decline in film sales, a constant challenge to meet debt commitments, continuous reductions in the workforce, and the continued low margins in the digital business.

Like Fisher, Perez wasn't given an easy hand to play – and this was made even trickier by a global recession that dented both consumer and business spending on its digital products. It is still unclear whether we are witnessing one of the greatest transformations in business history, or a slow-motion corporate car crash of epic proportions. The market, it has to be said, is veering towards the latter.

Where has it gone right?

There has been wave after wave of redundancies – tens of thousands of jobs have gone. The turnaround Perez heralded in the quote at the start of this chapter has taken longer to deliver and there are still doubters – but there are a number of factors that offer encouragement.

1   Generating cash from the remaining film business

Nearly a third of Kodak's revenues are in what it calls its Film, Photofinishing and Entertainment (FM&P) division, which includes everything from single-use cameras to the reels of film used for movies, or the souvenir photo services that grab a picture of you while you're screaming your way round a roller-coaster, and post-production services for film makers. And even now, after years of decline this division continues to make an important cash contribution to the business.

Sales here dropped by 24% in 2009, but the division actually increased its earnings. No-one is under any delusion about which direction this business is heading in – and while it looks at some potential for growth in the broader chemicals market (yes, that again), this is about generating as much cash as possible for as long as possible to help fund the long-term reinvention of the business.

2 A smaller, leaner company

Fisher found a business that was too bureaucratic, slow and hierarchical; and so did Perez. The difference is that by the time Perez joined, in 2003, the decline of the film market was very visible. Kodak Park is now the Eastman Business Park with space let out to a host of technology businesses. And the blowing up of one of the old Kodak buildings was used as a promotional opportunity for their new line in inkjet printers.

3 A strong graphical communications division

For more than a century, the 'yellow' box not only embodied Kodak's identity with the public, but it was also by far the largest of Kodak's profits. Businesses such as this which are dependent on a single successful product are great for Wall Street, but when that product tumbles, then so does the whole business with it.

In a converged world where there is constant competition, I suspect that the consumer sector is going to remain too competitive, but the health of Kodak lies with its graphical communications business.

❝ Kodak now has three divisions ❞ Kodak now has three divisions – other than FM&P, there is Graphical Communications, which offers professional printing services, and its consumer digital operation.

Kodak's commercial digital printing solutions are well positioned to take advantage of the digital disruption that is still happening here. Inkjet printing allows for smart customisation and personalisation of printed products. Kodak here has the potential to be a disruptor rather than experience disruption. This is now their big adjacency.

4 Marketing mojo

Jeff Hayzlett became Kodak's CMO in 2006 and stayed in the role until 2010. And in those four years he gave the brand its marketing mojo back. When he joined, he said the mood was so low in the marketing team that 'people didn't even want to invest in a new carpet, let alone a major campaign'.[11]

Hayzlett set about changing that with a high-profile sponsorship of *The Apprentice* on US television, and making a big deal of using social media. He rapidly became one of the most high-profile CMOs in Corporate America. *Fortune* magazine asked if he was really promoting anything other than himself, but a business like Kodak needed someone continuously popping their head above the parapet. The worst thing for them was invisibility, or any hint of a lack of confidence.

Kodak built its brand using the best marketing techniques of the 20th century: using mass market advertising to create an emotional connection between it and its consumers. It has now set about doing the same using the best tools of the 21st century – through the use of social media and smart product placement. It didn't just sponsor *Celebrity Apprentice*, but had Kodak products featured in episodes. At one point in the programme we had Stephen Baldwin explaining the virtues of Kodak's printers to his brother Alec: surreal but effective.

5 Fixing the balance sheet

Perez, like Fisher, has had to fix his balance sheet by exiting a market – in his case it was Health Imaging, which delivered a healthy stream of cash, but had limited growth potential.

In the summer of 2009, as questions were being asked about how long Kodak could keep losing money on a quarterly basis, Kodak announced a major refinancing with KKR. The terms of the deal are massively favourable to KKR, and there were plenty of angry share-holders. KKR secured a 10% income stream on their money (at a time of near zero interest rates), the best protection on the balance sheet,

---

11 In interview with the author.

and the potential to turn their warrants into 20% of the company should Kodak prosper.

But, the important thing is that this deal happened at all. It was the middle of the credit crunch. Banks weren't handing money out, and if something hadn't been done, the business would have been under ever greater pressure in the capital markets.

6 Better consumer products

There are still spectacular challenges for Kodak in the consumer technology market – but they are definitely bringing better products to market more quickly. They have focused their efforts on entry-level cameras that offer ease of use. Kodak also have a great range of low-end video cameras – which are easy to use, and offer fantastic quality for the price – but they have a very strong competitor here in Flip, which is now owned by Cisco.

The test, though, is whether their play in the printer market will work. They finally made their real launch here in 2007 – offering consumers a lower lifetime cost of ownership (basically cheaper ink) in exchange for a slightly higher up-front cost. They forecast that by 2011 the majority of sales here will be for ink, where the margins are spectacular, and as a result over time they will be expecting a 40% gross margin. We shall see.

The story of Kodak teaches us many things – not least the sheer effort required on the long road back to recovery after disruption has hit. They could and should have been more radical earlier – both in terms of cutting cost, and in delivering great digital products, even if they disrupted their core business: but even this, I suspect would not have affected their overall direction of travel over the past decade. The move to chemicals might have saved them – but they paid too much for the wrong business.

The real lesson though is that no matter how strong your business is, it is never truly safe. The challenge of ensuring your core business is as efficient as possible, and constantly looking for new adjacent markets, is always best tackled in relatively healthy times, rather than when you are dealing with a rapid, structural decline. A lesson that I hope has been heeded by the final sector we look at: the world of book publishing.

9

Out of print: the reinvention of book publishers

We can argue about speed and direction but there's not much doubt that the world of books is undergoing its most profound structural shift since Gutenberg. How will we book publishers respond to this opportunity? With anxious enthusiasm is the honest answer. (John Makinson, Penguin Group CEO, 2010)[1]

In July 1999, as the dotcom boom was getting into full swing, I took part in a debate in the *Guardian* titled 'Will the book be supplanted by electronic technology?' I was arguing 'Yes' against Brian Laing, then chief executive of the British Library. It was all rather contrived. I didn't believe then, and nor do I believe now, that the book was going to disappear. Laing, meanwhile, was no Luddite. He had led an impressive digitisation programme at the British Library and was excited about the way that the internet could encourage the flow of knowledge around the world. We skipped around the topic delicately and politely and reached little in the way of conclusion.

A decade on, as I prepare to become a microscopic part of the publishing industry, the first wave of devices that could in some way be thought of as replacements for books – the Kindle, the iPad, the

---

1 Quoted in 'Apple's IPad and the Evolution of Books', *Wall Street Journal*, 8 February 2010.

Nook and a host of others – are in our hands. And the debate that we had in the paper all those years ago, still rumbles on. As each new type of device appears, the same question gets asked: 'So, is this the end of the book?'

The much-hyped launch of Apple's iPad brought on another wave of such speculation. *Guardian* columnist, Simon Jenkins, a regular burster of neophiliac bubbles sprang to the defence of the printed word with rhetorical flourish:

Gutenberg has yet to be bettered. A book is an indestructible, self-sufficient product, its character reflecting the genius of one creative mind. As long as words are written and people can read, settling down with a book remains an intimate sharing of sensibility. It delights the eye, as a shelf of books furnishes a room. It offers escape from the ubiquitous screen.[2]

His column, however, like the debate I had a decade earlier, completely missed the point. Even if we are still reading books in their most traditional format a century from now, the arrival of the internet is bringing about a profound creative disruption in the publishing world – and for publishers the challenges of core transformation, edge innovations and finding big adjacencies are as real and urgent as in any other sector.

The delights of double disruption

The book industry – and I should stress that I'm predominately talking about consumer or 'trade' publishing here – is interesting because it was one of the first to experience the shift to online transactions of physical goods, a first wave of creative disruption sparked by Amazon. And now, after watching the newspaper and music industries, it is about to embark on its second wave as books turn into e-books.

2 Simon Jenkins (2010) 'Palms, Kindles, Nooks, iPads – none of them are as cool as Gutenberg's gadget', the *Guardian*, 29 January.

In little more than a decade, the internet has gone from a niche to the mainstream. It is now the largest channel for book sales in the US (with 23% share in 2008 just ahead of the 22% share of major chains), and it is heading that way in the UK, where the internet now accounts for 14% of sales. To add an extra twist, this move also coincided with supermarkets getting into book sales. In the UK, for example, Tesco went from being nowhere in the book world to taking 6% of the market by value, and 10% by volume by 2007.[3] Wal-Mart in the US showed a similar staggering growth. Their focus is on selling large volumes of relatively few books at dramatically reduced prices.

There are three big impacts from this first wave.

1 New, big powerful customers

There have been three very big impacts on the market as a whole. The first is that publishers internationally have had to get used to dealing with customers (as they call their retailers) whose scale, growth rate, and general level of ambition is unlike anything they have had to deal with before. These are not just bookstores – these are the most successful retailers in the world who happen to sell books.

❝ these are not just bookstores ❞

The relationship between publishers and Amazon has not always been the happiest – that is putting it mildly. During one row in the UK during 2008 between the retailer and Hachette, one of the largest publishers, Amazon took the 'Buy it new' buttons off all of Hachette's books. The publisher's CEO, Tim Hely Hutchinson, sent a letter to his authors summing up how many publishers see Amazon, saying the company 'seems each year to go from one publisher to another making increasing demands in order to achieve richer terms at our expense'.[4]

---

3 http://www.thebookseller.com/in-depth/feature/58753-tescos-giant-strides.html
4 From a leaked letter, http://caribbeanbookblog.wordpress.com/2010/02/05/amazon-apple-and-the-big-6-get-to-rumble-in-the-e-books-jungle/

2 Fewer bigger hits, and a long, long, long tail

The next impact has been a change in the make-up of the book market – and what we the public are buying. Amazon offers infinite shelf space, and it is easier than ever before for small publishers to get titles on there and build up nice audiences. The total number of books published in the UK in 2009 was the highest it had been for 15 years; with some 3,000 publishers putting out a book for the first time.[5]

At the same time, thanks heavily to supermarkets selling large volumes of a small number of books at dramatic discounts, the best selling books account for an ever-growing proportion of total sales. In the UK, sales of the ten best selling books were 3.4m in 1998 and 6m in 2008.[6]

The result has been an ever greater focus on the big hits – celebrity biographies, cookery books, and massive fiction franchises such as Harry Potter or the Twilight series; while mid-ranking authors have seen their advances cut, as retailers place smaller and smaller orders.[7] The much fabled 'long tail' is there – but there isn't a whole lot of money to be made there.

3 The decline of traditional retailers

The final impact has been to leave traditional retailers reeling. In the UK, the number of independent bookshops in the UK dropped by 30% over a decade according to the Booksellers Association.[8] Borders went into receivership, closing down 45 branches. And the market leading chain Waterstones saw profits decline despite dramatic cost reduction.

---

5 http://www.nielsenbookdata.co.uk/uploads/press/NielsenBook_
BookProductionFigures3_Jan2010.pdf
6 http://www.economist.com/displaystory.cfm?story_id=14959982
7 http://entertainment.timesonline.co.uk/tol/arts_and_entertainment/books/
article6684436.ece
8 'High Street loses two independent bookshops a week', *The Bookseller*, 8 February 2010, www.thebookseller.com/news

In the US, smaller retailers have felt a similar squeeze. When Amazon, Wal-Mart and Target all slashed the price of the top ten best selling hardbacks to $9 (from $25), the American Booksellers Association said they were 'devaluing the very concept of a book' adding that 'the entire book industry is in danger of becoming collateral damage in this war.'[9]

The next wave of disruption

This has been quite some upheaval then – the result of two of our four forces of disruption at play: the arrival of entrepreneurs into the market, and a consumer desire for more convenient and cheaper book buying.

In literary terms, however, this first decade was merely the exposition: an introduction to the main characters before the real action begins in the second act. And that second act is the digitisation of books: and with it comes, as I have described, a new physics of publishing.

Enter our third force of disruption: a proliferation of devices and services hitting the market in 2010 building on the early success of Amazon's Kindle. Apple has launched its iPad; Google has launched its online store Google Editions; and smart phones of every kind carry apps that allow you to read books on them. Some of them will, no doubt, sink without trace – but it would take a brave man to bet against significant growth in the e-book market over the next five years.

And yes, I suspect the economy – our fourth force – will also have a role to play here. Books have not been particularly cyclical purchases in the past, but consumer electronics are. The shift to e-books is only going to accelerate as the economy starts to pick up, consumer confidence rises and more e-readers and smartphones are sold.

---

9 'Walmart, Target, Amazon: Book Price War Heats Up', *Time Magazine*, http://www.time.com/time/business/article/0,8599,1932426,00.html

The result, I believe, is going to be an even more radical core transformation within the publishing world – as the models and methods for finding talent and creating value from it are reinvented piece by piece. The quote at the start of the chapter from Penguin's John Makinson shows how seriously some of the major publishers are treating this. But, if you look at some of the forecasts, the idea of the 'biggest structural shift since Guttenberg' might seem a little melodramatic.

66 it will still only be around 6% of the total market by 2013 99

In 2008, e-books accounted for only 1.5% of the global consumer book market according to PWC. They forecast that even after dramatic growth predicted in the next few years, it will still only be around 6% of the total market by 2013.

These bald statistics are enough to bring on a major wave of denial to those who are sceptically inclined. Why all the fuss if it is only going to be 6% of the market in three years' time? First, the data that started to appear around Christmas 2009 was that anything up to 30% of sales of big name titles at Amazon are now on the Kindle. Then in the summer of 2010, Amazon revealed it was selling more e-books than hardbooks.

'Once you go digital you don't go back,' Steve Haber, president of Sony's Digital Reading division said in the *Financial Times*, pointing out that once people got digital cameras, 'film did not re-emerge'.[10] Admittedly, he has a vested interest here – but the point is well made. Once you have an e-reader, or you download the Kindle app onto your iPhone, it becomes your book devouring tool of choice.

The heart of the problem: a new role in a new world

The sense of urgency from Makinson and his peers within the industry is driven by more than a disagreement over percentage points. It comes from an understanding that rather than debating the size,

10 David Gelles and Andrew Edgecliff-Johnson (2010) 'A Page is Turned', *Financial Times*, 9 February.

shape and speed of the arrival of the digital world, they need to get the foundations right, or it is going to be a toxic part of the business.

There is no good seeing a dramatic surge in e-book sales if the margins in the digital world are worse than in print or if the result is widespread piracy, or even worse if authors and their agents decide that in the digital world they don't actually need a traditional publisher. And this leads us to the publishers' nightmare scenario: disintermediation by big name writers.

Early in 2010, for example, the leading UK author Ian McEwan struck a deal that gave the exclusive digital rights for his back catalogue to Amazon. He has swapped a standard royalty of 25% for electronic books for one of nearly 50%. In July, agent Andrew Wylie signed an exclusive e-book deal directly with Amazon for his authors – cutting out the publishers.

The problem is that big names such as these provide the cash that helps to fund new authors. But they are also the people who can survive best without a big publisher – especially when it comes to the digital world. Without relatively predictable earners such as the back catalogue of big name authors, publishers' portfolios become that bit more volatile. Dangerously so in some cases.

It's true that if there are no printing, distribution and warehousing costs then there is room for improved margins. But everyone wants a slice: consumers want lower prices and authors want bigger royalties. But Makinson argued in the *Wall Street Journal* that those costs only make up some 10% of the total costs of a book and the business still has to maintain the fixed cost of its print infrastructure. So, when it comes to pricing and royalties, there is, he said, 'some room for discussion but not that much.'[11]

The point is clear: they cannot simply count on their big name authors coming with them into the digital world, and it seems clear

---

11 See note 1.

that one way or another, this is going to cost them. Given the tight margins that these businesses operate under, it is almost certain that this will result in cost reduction elsewhere: staff numbers and advances to mid-ranking authors are likely to come under pressure for some time yet.

So here is the first core transformation challenge within trade publishing: a need to re-establish the publishers' role as an intermediary and to deal with the negotiating might of Amazon, Apple and Google. And if there is a moment to negotiate this is it, while all the major players – especially Amazon, Apple and Google – are jockeying for position and there is some chance that they can be played off against each other.

This is why we saw a flurry of activity from Amazon at the time of Apple's iPad launch. The US chief executive of Macmillan, John Sargent, managed to negotiate a change in pricing model for books on the Kindle just after Apple announced it was launching the iBookstore. And the weeks before the iPad launch, publishers had been in ferocious negotiation with Apple to allow for higher prices on its new device: something they secured in exchange for being named part of the launch line-up.

But this transformation – of the business model of a straight transfer from selling physical books to digital ones – is just a start of the industry's likely revolution. Those who prefer big bold visions of the future will point to smart new models for selling books: particularly around subscription. The specialist technology publisher O'Reilly has had some success by allowing its technology books to become available for subscription under its 'Safari Books Online', which is relevant for a reference library but perhaps less so for mainstream fiction. But, even so, this to me is an edge innovation – the core challenge is trying to get the pricing and technology right for the main volume of sales with the largest retailers.

The science of hits

The other element of core transformation under way is in the discovery and development of talent. Book publishing is a hits business – and to put it crudely, the more hits you have, the healthier your business is going to be. The challenge is to be the best at finding and developing hit titles. This is part art, and part luck. Increasingly, though, thanks to the internet, there are ever smarter ways to find new talent.

The world of blogs has provided perfect source material for editors to not only find people who can write, but people who can publish with an established audience. The result has been authors whose voices might never have been heard. Belle de Jour was a blog by a then anonymous prostitute (later revealed to be a scientist using her night-time earnings to fund her PhD). At the *Guardian* we made it blog of the year in 2004, and after that her fame and notoriety spread. Eventually, the blog became a best-selling book and TV series.

❝ they have managed to create a genuine community ❞

HarperCollins has taken a slightly more systematic approach, turning its 'slush-pile' – the stack of rejected manuscripts – into the basis for a community for budding authors: Authonomy. com. People read then vote on their favourite manuscripts and the best titles end up being published. Already a number of bestsellers have come from this. It works because they have managed to create a genuine community that the members value.

At the moment, this too is a classic edge innovation. Authonomy is a great experiment, the question is whether it – or some aspect of it – could become a core part of the way that publishers work and select which manuscripts they want to invest in. After all, why anticipate the public's reaction to a work when you can measure it?

The internet is awash with data on trends and behaviour: from search trends to traffic on blogs, feedback from social networks, or comments on newspaper website articles. All are indicators of public sentiment that previously could only have been guessed at. All can be measured and monitored. All provide data where there were previously just hunches.

There is always going to be some level of art in working out what will sell, and how much you should invest in it. But, the shift in the make-up of books sales has made it harder and harder to take risks, and as a result there is going to be an ever-greater intrusion of science into this art of editorial selection. To be overly dependent on data is dangerous, but not to use what data there is out there is even more so.

The smarter publishing marketers are already appropriating the tactics of the likes of the big packaged goods manufacturers: with greater understandings of customer segments, using smart customer relationship management to move their readers from one author to the next, developing greater insight about which distribution channels will work best for which type of author. And as consumers start to buy books in different ways, through different devices and outlets, getting recommendations from friends on social networks rather than just reading reviews in newspapers and magazines, there is going to be a need to continuously challenge previous assumptions about 'the book-buying public'.

One of the lessons that book publishers can learn at the expense of newspaper and music industries is that consumers often shift their habits much faster than incumbent businesses would like.

Beyond books – and even e-books

With these two core functions in place it is also going to be vital for publishers to look beyond the simple digital replication of their books, into new screen-based formats, which I believe points towards the big adjacencies in the publishing market.

To give an example of how book publishing is evolving here, I spoke with Donna Hayes, the chief executive of Harlequin, the massively entrepreneurial Canadian publisher of romance titles (they own Mills & Boon in the UK) with $500m in annual sales. To her the digital world offers a wealth of opportunity to get 'more content, in more ways, to more women'.

In 2009, this digital activity accounts for around 6% of global sales – so they are already ahead of the market. By 2012, Donna thinks it will increase to around 15–20%. At a basic level, Harlequin have started to use e-readers to offer digital-only stories that might never have made it into print: erotic short-form literature – novellas of 20–30 pages – which are priced at $2.99. (Interestingly, the same tactic, at the same price point has been adopted by the publishers of this book, Pearson, who now release a series of 5,000–10,000 business briefings for e-readers at $2.99.)

But Harlequin are also developing new formats. In Japan, for example, their English romances are first translated into Japanese text, then converted by an artist into a Manga-style comic for print. These are then digitised, originally to go onto mobile phones in Japan but they have also found a new life as iPhone applications.

We have seen some similar developments in the world of children's books. Penguin and Egmont have teamed up with the games publisher Electronic Arts to develop *FLIPS* a version of children's books for the Nintendo DS, where the original text of, say, Enid Blyton's *Enchanted Woods*, containing a number of digital enhancements, is brought to the perfect platform for the target audience.

This is just the start. The experience from the world of business and scientific publishing is that it is possible to create value in the move to digital by creating workflow tools: effectively taking print-based content and using digital technology to create something that is much, much more useful. The example in Chapter 2 of an x-ray journal turned into a terminal-based service that is part of the radiographer's workflow is a good example of this. And I believe the same is going to be true with much consumer material, primarily through the development of mobile applications.

The obvious first steps here are travel guides and recipes; just two examples where books can be the core foundation of high-value applications that are aware of your location, some of your preferences and the time of year. The result can be much more useful – and therefore much more potentially valuable and profitable than a book.

Fighting for a place at the table

Yet again, the challenge for publishers here is that they are going to have to fight to be part of this process of value creation. The publishing world involves rights being split into formats and geographies and just because you get the right to publish someone's book, it doesn't give you the right to turn it into an iPhone app.

In 2009, for example, celebrity chef Jamie Oliver launched an iPhone app, *Jamie's 20 Minute Meals*, that showcased 50 recipes with some added functionality such as videos and a shopping list feature. The initial pricing at £4.99 was cheap compared to one of his books, but he could happily deliver one of these a month; or offer a subscription service. The point is that this was very much his application, created by the app developer Zolmo, without a traditional 'publisher' involved.

So yet again we face an element of digital disintermediation. If publishers are to seize the growth potential here they will have to build on their core advantages (their relationships with authors, and exposure to ideas, characters and properties at a very early stage) and enhance them with new skills, ventures and partnerships. Publishers need to go beyond books, and even e-books. Take the example of this book. When I first met with the publishers they warned me I wouldn't make much money from it, but there is money in public speaking. I was slightly taken aback then when they didn't immediately introduce me to their speaking agency. After all, why not reap the profits rather than hand them off to another intermediary?

❝ publishers need to go beyond books, and even e-books ❞

On a considerably more ambitious scale, Random House is looking to exploit the potential of its children's books by going into partnership with Komixx Entertainment to create a joint venture, Random House Children's Screen Entertainment, to develop cartoons, live action drama and games. Early in 2010, they announced their first deal – signing the worldwide film rights to *Monster Republic*, a teenagers' sci-fi book by the author Ben Horton. The deal was signed pre-publication – in other words they used their advance knowledge of the book and the author to their advantage – and was heralded by Philippa Dickinson of Random House as proof of how to develop a concept from manuscript to a multimedia platform.

This is not without its risks. Not every manuscript becomes a great book; and not every great book becomes a great film or computer game or mobile application. The potential for publishers to extract even greater value from the intellectual property they help create is balanced against the increase in risk that comes from moving into new creative forms and distribution channels. There will be plenty of failures from moves similar to those by Random House. That is part of the business. But, as we have seen, these are the challenges with all significant adjacency moves. And as with other experiences, there is an equal risk in not seeking them out if you want to deliver long-term growth through the process of digitisation.

Of all the sectors I have looked at while putting this book together, trade publishing is the one that is most in the balance. I suspect the uptake of e-books, either via dedicated readers such as the Kindle or the iPad, or through smartphones, will outstrip most forecasts. The devices are gorgeous, the experience for reading fiction or biography (basically anything that you don't dip in and out of) is perfect. In general digital adoption always outstrips most people's forecasts in the long run.

The challenge for publishers then is whether they have learned enough from watching the newspaper industry and the music industry, to be able to get the basics right from the outset. For the sake of the success of this very small drop in the publishing ocean, I sincerely hope they have.

Epilogue: what happens next?

n Chapter 2, I looked forward to the next wave of creative disruption and asked a set of questions about how things might change in the coming years. All of these questions still loom large; and I don't pretend to know the answers. To paraphrase Donald Rumsfeld, there is simply too much that we don't know we don't know.

If the internet has demonstrated anything over the past 15 years, it is an ability to deliver massive change at an unprecedented rate. If we go back to as recently as 2004, we find that Facebook had barely been born and Twitter didn't exist. YouTube, the BBC's iPlayer and Hulu weren't around. There was no Kindle. The idea that Apple might launch a mobile phone seemed to be pushing the very limits of credibility. Google's revenues for the year stood at $3bn; by 2009 they had grown to $23.6bn.

The flipside of this was that five years earlier things had felt much, much more comfortable within most incumbent businesses in the media industries and elsewhere. Newspapers, magazines, broadcasters all seemed challenged but resilient. But that too was going to change. At the Guardian Media Group we owned a portfolio of regional newspapers valued at the time at around £200m. By the time we sold them in 2010, the total value of the deal was less than £40m.

Even in a relatively short period this wave of creation and disruption was much more violent than anyone imagined. To try and make predictions about who will rise and who will fall against that backdrop would simply be faking certainty in an uncertain world.

But, even if we can't name the winners and losers of the next decade – we can be reasonably sure about the conditions.

More *Blade Runner* than *The Jetsons*

The Jetsons, you may remember, was a space age version of *The Flintstones* – set in 2062. Our hero, George Jetson, flew to work in his aerocar to spend three hours a day, three days a week pressing a single button at Spacely's Sprockets before going home to his futuristic apartment and a house full of holograms and labour-saving devices. Technological utopians tend to picture a world like *The Jetsons* – one where the past has effectively been eradicated, and we are just left with all that is shiny and new.

This view of the future is one where all remnants of the past have been erased and there is nothing but the future. However, this never happens. A much more accurate picture comes with *Blade Runner* – set in a dystopian Los Angeles in 2019. There is smart enough technology to develop replicants that looked and behave like humans; but the streets are still filthy. Half the world is gleaming, high-tech, the other is decaying and old.

This *Blade Runner*-like tension between old and new is already part of our world, and is going to be the defining characteristic of the decade ahead of us. Old businesses will continue to push themselves through wave after wave of transformation, fighting for survival, in some cases to the bitter end. New businesses will burst on the scene – some of them will be around for decades, some will last little longer than their launch party.

Incumbents of all kinds: fasten your seatbelts

We know too that there is still plenty of turbulent change ahead. The four driving forces of creative disruption: entrepreneurs, what people want and need, device proliferation, and economic volatility show no sign of abating. In particular, the spread of internet-connected mobile phones and televisions is likely to drive another wave of change in consumer behaviour.

The first Wi-Fi connected televisions are in the shops as I write this. Within a few years, this will be standard functionality. Similarly, Nielsen has predicted there will be more smartphones than mobile phones in the USA from 2011. In other words, technologies that were only for the earliest of early adopters a few years ago are now working their way into the mainstream – and with it, the internet is working its way out from the PC and into pretty much every electronic device we own. This will combine with an upturn in the economy that will make life easier for everyone, but will disproportionately favour digital businesses: economic gravity is on their side.

❝ economic gravity is on their side ❞

The incumbent businesses that have been most shaken by creative disruption already will continue to be challenged. They have entered a new reality of almost constant evolution and change; and the hope that things might soon 'go back to normal' is dangerously flawed. This is the new normal.

'Stability' as businesses once knew it will only return when they have a business that has the same sort of protection that they once experienced. For most of them, however, there is little sign of this happening. For those who work in these businesses, and hear how much simpler things used to be, there will be a constant sense of being the ones who have had to tidy up after the party.

The record labels, newspapers, retailers, directory businesses, ad agencies and publishers that succeed in the coming years will do so because they continue to reinvent themselves around a strong core sense of purpose. Those who have not already set about transforming their core businesses, and searching for big adjacent markets where they can find growth, will find themselves slipping further behind. There will be casualties as a result.

Who's next?

At the same time the twin whirlwinds of creation and disruption will hit other sectors. Clayton Christensen, who defined the notion of disruption in the first place, has turned his attention to the worlds of education and healthcare – where, in both cases, consumers are getting direct access to technology and information that previously could only be accessed via professionals. Joe Schoendorf, the veteran Silicon Valley venture capitalist, similarly sees an unprecedented wave of change as well: 'You look at what's going on in the valley right now,' he says, 'we used to have two or three schemes of disruption, now we have about a dozen.'[1]

As I write this, barely a day goes by without someone writing about potential disruption in the energy business. A small army of start-ups are currently working on solutions to give consumers greater control of where they get their energy from, and how they regulate their use of it.

It is not only traditional physical businesses that will find themselves challenged. As we have seen with Yahoo! and MySpace, success in one wave of the internet is no guarantee of success in the next wave. Even Google knows it has to keep moving if it is going to grow – hence its moves into applications and the broader digital advertising market.

Amazon is a brilliant business: continuously restless and innovative. Their mastery of the physical logistics involved in their core business of moving books and DVDs around the world gives them a significant competitive advantage and creates barriers to entry. However, they are not beyond structural challenge. As those businesses become increasingly digital, the barriers to entry will drop. They will find themselves in pitched battles with Apple (already under way) and Google, and others who will launch pure digital bookstores and movie services, without the fixed cost base of warehousing required for storing physical goods.

---

1 Speaking at DLD, Hamburg 2010.

For every disruptive action, there is a creative reaction. And all of this provides opportunities for new entrants and entrepreneurs across the planet. While record labels grapple with the constant transformation of their business, smart players in the music business will build new types of businesses – similar to record labels, but with skills and expertise focused primarily on where the money is: helping big acts with live music, penetration into China and India, sponsorship revenues and music publishing.

The decline of digital squeamishness

As I have said repeatedly, it takes consumers and clicks to make this happen, and one of the reasons that we *can* be sure about the process of creative disruption continuing is the gradual decline of digital squeamishness – or an inherent resistance to doing things online.

At a simple level, we have seen consumers happily accessing their media digitally – initially newspapers and music, increasingly it will be movies and – as e-readers evolve – books and magazines. But, we have already gone way beyond that. One of the great changes to have happened over the previous five years has been the rise in the social acceptability of internet dating. Once seen as the last refuge of the truly desperate, it is now a completely acceptable – and effective – way to find a partner than heading out to a bar in the hope of finding Mr or Ms Right.

In other words, our single most important interpersonal 'transaction' – how we find the person we are hoping to spend the rest of our life with – is now happily carried out online. Once you have found your future husband over the internet, you will think nothing of finding a dress or booking a holiday. This way, the process of more people spending more time doing more things online will proceed, and with it, the migration from the physical to the digital economy and all of the upheaval that brings with it.

Contra vim mortis ...

When I first came up with the idea for this book, in the middle of 2007, I had a much more benign view of the prospects for most incumbent businesses. I suspect this was fuelled by working within the newspaper industry, and desperately trying to carve out the best digital future for our business. In particular, I felt that innovation, and smart, digital creativity could ultimately see you through. I was wrong. As I have stressed throughout these pages, nothing but radical reinvention is going to help those on the wrong side of creative disruption.

Great brands, smart people and a deep understanding of the digital world will help you take a peek over the wall to the future, but they won't guarantee you entry. That takes the hard slog of transforming your core business, and finding new growth markets.

For some, this simply isn't going to be possible. Perhaps they have left it too late; perhaps their balance sheets are just too weak to fund any real transformation; or perhaps their owners would rather just milk the business for cash while they can. These businesses will disappear. As the Latin saying goes: *Contra vim mortis, medicanem non est in hortis* – There is no cure for death in the garden. But as I hope I have shown, there is hope for those who have the right mix of vision and tenacity – those who can see the wealth of opportunities that are opening up, but realise that they are going to have to fight like never before to seize them. It is challenging. It is tough and often thankless work. But the reward is a ticket to a very exciting future – and that is surely well worth fighting for.

❝ the reward is a ticket to a very exciting future ❞

Index